ADVANCE PR*...*

"Based on a changing world, this book examines the act of leadership for years to come. Traversing the boundaries of culture, meaning-driven development, psychological safety, sustainability, design thinking, teamwork and decision making, Østergaard delivers a deep and broad perspective of future leadership. *Teal Dots in an Orange World* is a cornucopia of models, overviews, illustrations and reflection exercises combined with cases taken from some of our time's largest organizations in the domestic market. This book is best suited for large and ambitious organizations, but it can be read by anyone who wants a sneak peek into the future before it gets serious."

Alexandra Krautwald, Managing Director, advisory board member, keynote speaker, author and member at expert panel, Børsen Ledelse

"Erik Korsvik Østergaard's new book carries on where his last book ended with an increased understanding of the changes happening in management and organizational design. There is a need for change since many systems are hindered by old, hierarchical, linear and cultural baggage that has to find new forms in a world where fundamental structures are changing. Humanity, empathy and creativity are the way forward. Erik gives a strong input on how you can actively work on finding your own way in creating meaning and coherence for yourself as a leader, for your employees, your organization, your stakeholders and the outside world. Five teal stars to Erik's new book."

Jesper Rønnow Simonsen, Director and mentor

"An actionable, educational and refreshing book on how you can change organizations for better results while focusing on the areas of business that matter."
Garry Ridge, CEO, WD-40 Company

"A very practical and modern approach to building future organizations."
Jacob Morgan, Author, *The Future Leader: 9 Skills and Mindsets to Succeed in the Next Decade*

"Erik helps you think about how an organization can flourish by applying a modern leadership mindset. The combination of his findings and the work of other visionaries is a recipe for organizational transformation."
Matthew Gonnering, CEO, Widen

"This book provides an insightful and practical approach for creating more humanized organizations. I warmly welcome it!"
Professor Vlatka Hlupic, Author, *The Management Shift* and *Humane Capital*

"Many don't have the power the top boss has, but they can nevertheless stir the revolutionary embers by giving people a chance to experience being an adult at work – to own their work, to take command of it, and make it meaningful. I am very happy to see Erik's follow up to his *The Responsive Leader*. It reflects the fact that this movement will continue to evolve as it grows. In the words of Lisa Gill, 'enjoy the road because there's no finish line'."
Matt M. Perez, COO and co-founder, Nearsoft

TEAL
DOTS
IN AN ORANGE WORLD

HOW TO ORGANIZE THE WORKPLACE OF THE FUTURE

ERIK KORSVIK
ØSTERGAARD

Published by
LID Publishing Limited
The Record Hall, Studio 204,
16-16a Baldwins Gardens,
London EC1N 7RJ, UK

info@lidpublishing.com
www.lidpublishing.com

A member of:

BPR
Business Publishers Roundtable

www.businesspublishersroundtable.com

Printed in the Czech Republic by Finidr
ISBN: 978-1-912555-40-6

Cover and page design: Caroline Li

TEAL
DOTS
IN AN ORANGE WORLD

HOW TO ORGANIZE THE WORKPLACE OF THE FUTURE

ERIK KORSVIK
ØSTERGAARD

MADRID | MEXICO CITY | LONDON
NEW YORK | BUENOS AIRES
BOGOTA | SHANGHAI | NEW DELHI

CONTENTS

ACKNOWLEDGMENTS

So many people inspire me, challenge me and encourage me to pursue our journey and continue our investigation of the world of modern leadership and the future of work. This book is a product of our numerous genuine and mind-bending conversations, which I value deeply. I find myself blessed to have met and engaged with you.

Gorm Priem at ProActive, without whom this book would not have had the same focus. Our coffee meeting at Andersen & Maillard in September 2018 kept me moving with strong inertia. Thank you!

Perry Timms, for all our jams and ping-pong sessions on Skype and Slack, and for joining hands with us in Bloch&Østergaard towards a better, brighter future of work. You truly are an inspiration.

Louise Dinesen, Alexandra Krautwald and Christian Ørsted, for your deep engagement in modern, sustainable organizations, interpersonal mechanisms and psychological safety and insisting on debating and boosting the human aspects of the modern workplace and of balanced leadership.

Jesper Rønnow Simonsen, for our profound conversations on leadership and for insisting on challenging the existing mechanisms and habits.

Susanne Hoeck, for always cheering me on and connecting me with people, organizations and challenges, to the benefit of both parties.

Jeppe Vilstrup Hansgaard at Innovisor, for keeping on pushing the boundaries, and for analysing and exploiting the inner workings of organizational networks.

Thomas Gammelvind and Michael Bruun Ellegaard at Trustworks; Pia Verdich, Susanne Bork Klussmann and Michael Biermann at Ørsted; Camilla Hillerup at Microsoft Denmark; and Kent Højlund at Pingala, for opening your world and organizations for all of us to be inspired from. It is truly a phenomenal honour to have got to know your approach and learning.

Arbresh Useini, Guri Hanstvedt and Puk Falkenberg at Bloch&Østergaard, for your unlimited support, never-ending wondering and questions, hard work, humour and optimism, and for insisting on having a meaningful workplace with impact.

And, last but not least, Line Bloch, my business partner and wife, for fruitful collaboration and energizing encouragement, and for joining forces with me to create organizations where people want to show up for work.

MY AIM WITH THIS BOOK

This book is written for leaders like Berit and Jens Jakob, who are forward-thinking top-middle managers driving the development of modern organizations and progressive leadership.

And for leaders like Thomas and Jane, who struggle to introduce new management mechanisms into their bureaucratic worlds.

This is a follow-up to my first book, *The Responsive Leader* (Østergaard, 2018) – a sequel that needed to be written.

Since the publication of that book, I've given approximately 100 presentations, appeared in several podcasts, written more than 50 articles and been involved in a dozen organizational transformation programmes in Danish international corporate organizations. During those activities I have come very close to executive leaders in their own contexts, both in their management teams and as individuals – and I have discovered and codified four crucial lessons about their embrace of the future of work. The content and message of this book reflect these observations, correlated with my nearly 20 years of working in corporate enterprises.

The title of this book refers to the work done by Frédéric Laloux in his 2014 book *Reinventing Organizations*, where he describes five organizational stages in colours (Red, Amber, Orange, Green and Teal). Orange is the classical corporate structure; teal is the modern team-oriented organism. Throughout this book, I refer to these colours and build on the work of Laloux in a simple-to-understand, simple-to-apply language for leaders, to make a frame of reference that everybody can relate to and transmit.

Whereas my first book, *The Responsive Leader* (Østergaard, 2018), set the scene, describing the paradigm shift towards the future of leadership, *Teal Dots in an Orange World* addresses how to create that ecosystem in large corporate organizations:

- The design of Teal Dots (small teams)
- The design of the modern Orange World (minimal corporate support)
- How to distribute projects and activities in a new way
- How to redesign the corporate rhythm
- How to handle the space and network between teams
- How to master and lead the elements of the ecosystem
- Which leadership skills and capabilities are needed
- How to design the paradigm shift and execute it
- And thus: how to handle tactical execution in an ever-changing world

This book also builds on the term 'network of teams', coined by Deloitte (2017), and on the work of Gary Hamel and others, aiming at removing corporate bureaucracy.

This book describes how to design and transform your corporate business unit from command and control to network of teams on a tactical level. Ultimately, my aim is to describe new ways of working in a changed business world, where the debate of the modern mindset *has* taken place, and where we need to get the energy flowing to establish sustainable leadership and sustainable organizations.

I hope you'll be inspired to create organizations where people want to show up.

Erik Korsvik Østergaard

No man is an island, entire of itself;
every man is a piece of the continent,
a part of the main.

If a clod be washed away by the sea,
Europe is the less,
as well as if a promontory were,
as well as if a manor of thy friend's
or of thine own were.

Any man's death diminishes me,
because I am involved in mankind;
and therefore never send to know
for whom the bell tolls;
it tolls for thee.

———

John Donne,
poet, priest, and lawyer (1572–1631)
"Meditation XVII",
from *Devotions upon Emergent Occasions*, 1624

Culture and fellowship

INTRODUCTION AND STRUCTURE OF THE BOOK

This book is about leadership.

Well, obviously it is written with the design of modern, progressive, sustainable organizations in mind and as the narrative fixpoint, but it is a book about modern, progressive, sustainable leadership too.

There is no doubt that the business world is undergoing interesting and massive changes in these decades. The drivers are the technological advances – especially digitalization and the internet – and societal development and new expectations around engagement, sustainability and humanism.

Consequentiality, one of the strongest business trends is the paradigm shift in leadership towards a more people-oriented, meaningful and adaptive style. More collaborative and humane approaches combined with an ambitious drive for impact and results characterize this new way of leading.

Many leaders are aware of this development and know that they need to change their mindset, approach and habits. According to a survey by the Danish Association of Managers and Executives, 69% of the nearly 1,000 respondents know they need to change but are uncertain how to and what to change (Lederne, 2018).

However, progress *is* being made. Several leadership teams *are* frontrunners and spearheads and are driving transformation programmes and individual development projects to adapt themselves and their organizations to the new business world. They work with developing their mindset and approach to modern leadership and the future of work. They transform their focus from profit maximization to impact. They believe in innovation and experiments and are not afraid to embrace mistakes. They develop and nurture a culture of relationships and fellowship, of belonging and identity, of reflection and feedback, and of high-frequent touchpoints.

THE REAL CHANGE HAPPENS WHEN YOU TRANSFORM YOUR ORGANIZATION

The pivotal change happens when the leaders start reorganizing and redesigning how people work. Your effort and focus on leadership can only take you so far. Once you engage in redesigning your organizational structure and mechanisms, a massive release of energy takes place and lifts your organization into a totally new league.

The reason for this is threefold.

First, your organizational structure is a physical manifestation of the leadership that you practice. How you think and act when it comes to leadership and culture is directly mirrored in how you draw, design and orchestrate your business and its teams.

Second, your organizational structure is perceived by the employee as how the leadership treats them. Are we put into boxes with little to no room for creativity and individual decision-making, or are we set free and encouraged to think for ourselves? Are we organized for steadiness or for development? For predictability or for adaptability?

Third, once you engage in organizational transformation – or, less dramatically, in local reorganizations – your full spectrum of modern leadership skills is put into action. By engaging actively and deliberately in a reorganization, you have the opportunity to apply and sharpen your capabilities, reflect and learn even more, perform fantastic on-the-spot change management, and engage your employees in creating an organization where they want to show up.

The reorganization as an activity is an overlooked opportunity for great change management, great leadership development, great cultural coherence and great organizational engagement.

The more active, authentic and responsive leadership you practice, the more alignment between the intended leadership and the mirroring culture you will find. Your organizational design is a means and a medium for getting there.

ADAPTABILITY IS THE COMBINATION OF AUTONOMY AND ALIGNMENT

Several experiments with new ways of working indicate that the ability to stay relevant to employees and to the market comes from two elements: small autonomous teams and an ecosystem that interconnects the teams in alignment with each other.

> **Adaptability** comes from having a **sustainable ecosystem** of small autonomous teams, which together can shape the organization towards the new situation, in **alignment**.
>
> An **ecosystem** is a community of living organisms in conjunction with the non-living components of their environment, interacting as a system.

Experience shows that modern practices such as sociocracy, agile, lean startup and teal organizations present a solution to the first part, autonomy. However, scaling that approach up to corporate businesses with say 1,000 or 20,000 employees in alignment is a challenge.

This is where this book enters the scene.

The first of several 'How Might We' questions in this book is: How might we organize the workplace of the future with small, progressive teams; an ecosystem that interconnects those teams; and a modern, dynamic corporate platform that supports this? How might we create a design that scales to 20,000 employees?

WHO HAS THE ABILITY TO CHANGE THE BUSINESS WORLD?

New winds are blowing in the business world. The millennial mindset of purpose, freedom at work, impatience, ambition and a will to change the world is what carries us ahead. However, that approach is not confined to a specific generation or age group. It's a mindset, not a generation thing, and that is exactly what we need in the change agents, role models and influencers that drive this transformation.

The leaders today who have the greatest opportunity are characterized by three things.

First, they have a millennial mindset.

Second, they have a foot in both camps. They have experienced both the old, command-and-control business world and the epiphany of the new, progressive modern world.

Third, they have personal insight and reflect often. They are curious and courageous. They listen with the intent to understand and have a will to drive ambitious transformations.

This is a book about modern organizations, but it is a book about modern, sustainable, progressive leadership too.

THE STRUCTURE OF THIS BOOK

Using the approach of design thinking, we dive into the first of the two diamonds, 'designing the right thing', in order to allow for you to 'design the things right' in your context.

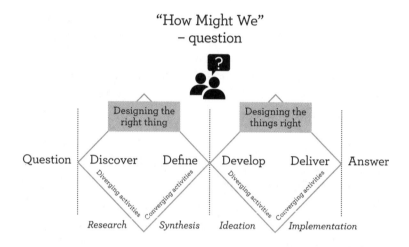

How Might We questions will be used several times in this book.

The book consists of four parts:

Part One: New ways of thinking describes four observations about the future to come. It presents a number of new and progressive organization designs in order to frame the understanding of Teal Dots in an Orange World.

Part Two: New ways of working challenges a popular approach to modern grand-scale organizations and instead formulates the right question and answer to be investigated in order to design modern, progressive organizations that are scalable and adaptable. It introduces the nine elements that go into building modern organizations for the future.

Part Three: New ways of leading gathers the findings from working with the four observations and the nine elements for building the modern Orange World. It describes the ecosystem, the paradigm shift in leadership that is needed and the organizational change management that fits with it.

Part Four: Practices and mechanisms showcases real-life approaches to building and maintaining the dynamics of modern organizations.

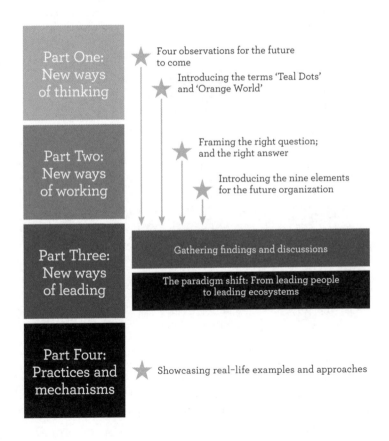

Part One:
New ways
of thinking

Four observations for the future
to come

Introducing the terms 'Teal Dots'
and 'Orange World'

Part Two:
New ways
of working

Framing the right question;
and the right answer

Introducing the nine elements
for the future organization

Part Three:
New ways
of leading

Gathering findings and discussions

The paradigm shift: From leading people
to leading ecosystems

Part Four:
Practices and
mechanisms

Showcasing real-life examples and approaches

The narrative is supported with case studies from four selected progressive Danish organizations: Microsoft Denmark, Ørsted, Pingala and Trustworks.

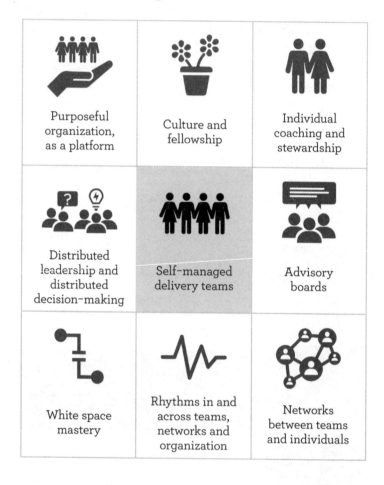

A central element in the book is the introduction and description of these nine elements of the future organization. Elaboration will be provided in Part Two, and they are presented here to give you a reference point and a help for reading.

I want to lead the organization,
but not lead the employees.

I don't want to steer.

I want to create the ability for
the employees to steer, when needed.

————

Kent Højlund,
CEO, Pingala A/S

Distributed leadership and
distributed decision-making

PART ONE:
NEW WAYS OF THINKING

Part One:
New ways
of thinking

Four observations for the future
to come

Introducing the terms 'Teal Dots'
and 'Orange World'

Part Two:
New ways
of working

Framing the right question;
and the right answer

Introducing the nine elements
for the future organization

Part Three:
New ways
of leading

Gathering findings and discussions

The paradigm shift: From leading people
to leading ecosystems

Part Four:
Practices and
mechanisms

Showcasing real-life examples and approaches

This part describes four observations about the future to
come. It presents a number of new and progressive organization designs in order to frame the understanding of Teal
Dots in an Orange World.

CHAPTER 1.
A NEW WORLD MEANS NEW PROBLEMS

There is no doubt that a paradigm shift in leadership and business is both needed and ongoing. Massive and unprecedented changes are taking place, fuelled by developments in technology and society.

As Gary Hamel states it, change itself has changed, as we are looking into a future with more changes, rapid changes and pivotal changes in technology, information and structures (Hamel, 2011). A vast number of surveys and studies have documented the reasons for, and effects of, these megatrends. Of course, lots of books have been written on Industry 4.0, disruption and the internet age, my own included.

The progressive executive leaders I've worked with over the past years all strive to be curious and experiment with their leadership and their ways of working. They have all concluded that if they continue with what they are doing – and how they do it – they will very soon not be relevant to the market or to their employees. I hear statements such as, "We used to be able to plan three years ahead. Now we plan for three months," "The new generations need both clear guidance and no limitations" and "We need to work like startup companies to keep up with the technology and our competitors. We need to transform our way of working."

The leaders do not only see the dystopian road forward. They also see possibilities and opportunities that they want to exploit. They see that the development will make it possible for them to create organizations that are healthier, fun to be part of, sustainable, antifragile and resilient to changes.

These leaders are inspired by the notions of flat organizations, Scrum and agile, lean startup, team of teams and the so-called 'wirearchies' – organizations that consist of tightly connected networks (Husband, 2015). They want to build and work in organizations that are vibrant and creative places.

The challenge is that all those leaders see the new problems, but they do not have the relevant tools in place to solve them.

THE PHILOSOPHY OF MODERN LEADERSHIP

Modern leadership at the beginning of the 21st century is characterized by a clear shift away from the qualities that dominated the workplace after the Second World War.

This leadership development is a response to seemingly dysfunctional management disciplines and to a management habit and narrative that are out of sync with the contemporary world.

New technology and massive development in societal expectations have set a new scene for leadership. Five principles guide leaders in navigating and driving their organizations:

1. People first
2. Purpose, meaning, sense-making and value creation
3. Continuous innovation and experimentation
4. An insatiable drive for results
5. Everybody has the opportunity to take a lead

Leadership is not a zero-sum game. Modern leadership behaviour is shaped by a sustainable approach to leadership, to the organization, to the community and to society. The four Ps characterize this balanced and holistic mindset and behaviour.

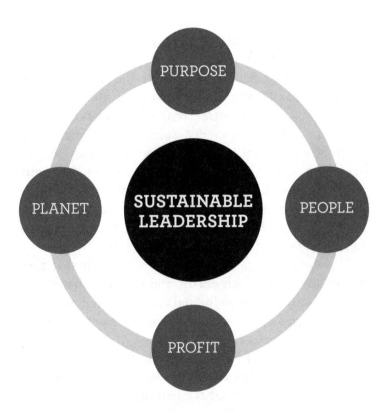

*Sustainable Leadership balances purpose, people,
the planet and profit, and understands and exploits
the synergies and correlations between them.*

Modern leaders evaluate their success not in terms of profit and market share alone, but also in terms of relationships, seeing other people grow, value creation and social capital. This is the new, modern triple bottom line. Such leaders believe in going well financially and doing good for the world. And they strive to create organizations where they themselves want to show up, day after day.

The philosophy is balanced, humanistic and sustainable, and based on the thought of connectedness: no man is an island.

THE PROACTIVE LEADERS WANT TO
CREATE THEIR FUTURE

Clearly, we need new tools to solve the new problems. However, not all leaders are aware of their situation.

In 2018, the Danish Association of Managers and Executives, Lederne, conducted a survey to investigate the challenges of digitalization and new technology for the role of the leadership (Lederne, 2018). Out of the nearly 1,000 respondents, 72% said that digitalization had already meant changes in their processes and value chain, while 41% reported changes in how they organized themselves and 39% reported changes in their own role.

However, only half of the respondents felt that they were ready to face such drastic and frequent changes. In the survey, they rated traditional areas like employee motivation, process optimization and management of work as the top three focus areas. In contrast, the bottom three focus areas in the Lederne (2018) report – emotional intelligence, agile development mechanisms and new ways of organizing – are predicted as emerging areas by the World Economic Forum (2018).

As the survey found, the less you focus on the future and on the world around you, the fewer challenges and opportunities you see. If you keep your head down, you don't see any risks. Twenty-five per cent of the leaders in the survey did not expect changes to their role. Twenty-five per cent!

During the conversations I have had with leaders and management teams over the years, I have come to realize that they tackle predictions about the future very differently. They fall into two camps, just as the survey from Lederne revealed: those who are reactive and wait for changes to happen to them, and those who take a proactive part in creating the future for themselves and their organization.

The first group, the reactive leaders, mostly continue their agendas as if tomorrow will be the same as yesterday. They have heard and seen what they refer to as 'doomsday prophecies of the future' too often; these prophecies have been made loudly but seemingly have no relevance to their own business.

The second group, the proactive leaders, is much smaller than the first group. They want to take an active part in creating the future, in creating the kind of organization they want to be part of themselves. They have choices to make, and they are not afraid of standing out in the crowd and experimenting with their strategy, their tactical execution, their approach to innovation, their uncompromising approach to culture and identity, and their own leadership style.

NEW PROBLEMS CALL FOR NEW SOLUTIONS

The leaders and management teams that successfully master the paradigm shift to the future of work do one thing that is different from the other proactive leaders. **They change their organization too**. Without doubt, organizations that redesign how they structure themselves *in alignment with* the modern mindset and behaviour are successful with their transformational leadership.

> Organizations that redesign how they structure themselves in alignment with the modern mindset and behaviour are successful with their transformational leadership.
>
> Redesign without mindset: unsuccessful
> Mindset without redesign: unsuccessful
> Redesign with mindset in place: successful

Undoubtedly, we need to solve the challenges and problems by designing organizations that are based on new characteristics. New problems call for new tools. In my view and in the eyes of the progressive leaders mentioned above, this is the answer to the challenges of a changed world: redesign your organization and embrace new ways of working.

Command-and-control

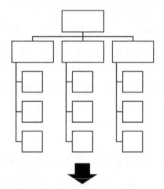

Command of teams

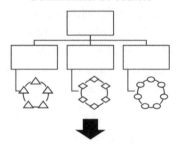

Team-of-teams

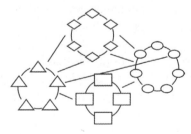

However, this is in harsh contrast to the existing hierarchical and functional organizational structures, built to optimize, control and streamline production. The classical organizations are designed to deliver predictable output, and this approach clashes with a need to fit into a VUCA world. The term 'VUCA' originated in the US Army War College in the 1990s in programmes on strategic leadership, and is an acronym used to describe or reflect on the volatility, uncertainty, complexity and ambiguity of general conditions and specific situations.

Out of the many different new experimental organizational structures, **the self-managed organization, team-of-teams structures** and **agile/Scrum** are the predominant ones. In 2016, 2017 and 2018, Deloitte documented the development of these organizational structures in three reports indicating the skills and dynamics needed to make these structures possible (Deloitte, 2016, 2017, 2018).

Other types of leadership and organizational structures were covered in the reports too, but these three – self-management, team of teams and agile/Scrum – were the most mentioned, but also the most elusive and perhaps even mythical. The following are paraphrased quotes from leaders that illustrate the perception of these organizational designs as the solution to all problems:

"Spotify does it! If we just apply Scrum and Enterprise Agile to our company in the same way, we'll be sure to deliver the right things at the right time, all the time."

"Look at Zappos, Morningstar, Medium, Patagonia or Buurtzorg. They have eliminated managers and are fully based on self-managed teams. We want that."

"Holacracy or sociocracy – that is the answer."

"We are an Orange organization. We want to be Teal."

The truth is that the halos of these narratives seem to out-shine the real stories, including the struggles involved in applying these modern approaches to large, existing corporate structures. They do not fit well in all situations. They are often hard to scale. And implementation and embracement are way harder than anticipated, as changing habits in large corporate institutions is tremendously slow and takes years.

I believe that the answer is to follow these steps:
1. Get the mindset in place
2. Use inspiration from the self-managed teams
3. Redesign the organization and your platform
4. Find your way to scale it – and lead it

But how do you do this? Steps 1 and 2 seem manageable in small organizations and have been successful. Studies show that. Steps 3 and 4, the redesign and scaling part, are the toughest. How do you turn a business unit with 150 employees around? Or an organization with 10,000 employees, distributed across several locations and in several cultures and time zones?

A PARADIGM SHIFT IN LEADERSHIP FOCUS
OF THE FUTURE OF WORK

As I documented in my first book, *The Responsive Leader* (Østergaard, 2018), the leadership of the future is dramatically different from what we were trained in mastering in the latter half of the 20th century.

New leadership needs to be less top management, more delegation. Less planning, more experimentation. Less command and control, more coaching and emotional intelligence. Less 'you go to work', more 'you belong here'. Less focus on products and output, more focus on problem-solving and outcome.

Getting things done in the future world will be heavily influenced by two megatrends: massive invasion of technology in the workplace and an increasing focus on humanism at work. Both parts affect how leaders can and should act. These can be termed 'high tech' and 'high touch'.

High tech means exploiting digital advantages in research, collaboration (also with external organizations and more vaguely defined groups online) and communication. It's the idea of using technology and especially digital tools to support dialogue, transparency, wellbeing, performance and value creation on an individual level and in teams.

High touch means genuinely caring for employees, customers and the planet, using emotional intelligence and humanism to get the right balance between privacy and professionalism. Understanding sustainable leadership and serving the needs of people, planet, purpose and profit are essential for transforming organizations and engaging people.

FOUR OBSERVATIONS ABOUT A FUTURE TO COME

New ways of working are coming at you, whether you want them or not and whether you are ready or not. The paradigm shift is inevitable and driven by massive changes in technology and society, and every leader should be aware of this. However, only a fraction of leaders are proactive and try to create the world they want to be a part of. The rest are reactive, hoping either that the changes will turn out to be a fad or that someone else will fix the problem while they keep their head down and focus on efficiency and productivity.

I have observed these four mechanisms in progressive organizations that set them apart from the rest:

1. **Getting extraordinary things done in the modern corporate world happens in small teams only**, not in large operational structures. This observation is unrelated to the size and impact of the organization. Success is not an attribute of corporate collaboration but of small, self-managed, self-propelled teams in a team-of-teams structure in a universe of minimal corporate support.

2. **Work happens in highly connected networks of leaders**, subject matter experts, internal influencers and corporate team players with high emotional intelligence. The old way of designing the hierarchical organization is counter-productive and alienating to progressive leaders and employees, and not fitting for a business world that calls for change, adaptation, cross-organizational collaboration and distributed decision-making. Instead, those leaders who design their organization in a circle-like fashion (like pearls on a necklace, a Venn diagram, a flower with petals or similar) convey the message of collaboration and participative leadership in a vital and pivotal way.

3. **Tactical execution happens when touchpoints are frequent and physical**, and when the rhythm of the business unit or department is synchronous across the team of teams. This implies a radical new approach to calendar control, as a new set of meetings must be embraced, replacing the existing 'investigate and report' meeting culture. This new way of working consists of more frequent touchpoints, with shorter durations and new purposes for meeting.

4. **The reorganization as an activity is a pivot point for transformational leadership**. Two aspects are at play here. First, when it is done well, the reorganization is a melting pot and opportunity for activating and aligning your leadership and culture beyond the theory and training and across the organization. Second, small and frequent reorganizations will serve your organization well when it comes to embracing and supporting change and even pivotal disruptions. Together, this enables the emergence of transformational leadership.

These four mechanisms are the building blocks for scaling the progressive, modern organizational formats from a single team or a few teams to massive business units.

The approach is:

- Those who change their mindset can change their organization
- Those who change their organization have success with their transformation
- The new organizational structures work, but mostly on a small scale
- Changing the large organization is incredibly hard
- Four mechanisms set the progressive organizations and leaders apart from the rest

Together, this framework paves the way for autonomy in teams, alignment between teams, and an adaptable, sustainable, connected organization.

Let's get to work.

CHAPTER 2.

TEAL AND ORANGE:

A NEW LANGUAGE FOR CULTURE AND DYNAMICS

This chapter highlights the megatrends, management thinking and organizational philosophies that are prevailing and setting the agenda for the modern approach to work and organizations:
- The emergence of self-governance
- Sociocracy and organizational democracy
- Teal and Orange as reference terms

The goal here is to establish the terms 'Teal' and 'Orange' as umbrella concepts to give you and your leadership team a mutual language to debate your organizational design.

THE EMERGENCE OF SELF-MANAGEMENT

In the second half of the 20th century, a bunch of alternative and redesigned approaches to organizational design arose. These emerging structures grew as a response to perceived unnecessarily tight control, polarization, unfairness and inequality, and a seemingly mechanistic and functional approach to the workplace. As with many other radical inventions, discoveries and movements, they saw the light of day simultaneously in parallel in several places across the globe.

The shared characteristic and design principle of these movements is the human approach to work. This does not mean that work or the workplace should be a humanitarian construct, but that the individual worker should have a great job at a great workplace, with fairness and dignity.

According to these movements, organizations should be based on shared principles, namely **shared purpose**, **self-governance** and **social capital** (see Agile Alliance, 2001; Kolind and Bøtter, 2012; Ries, 2011; and ConsciousCapitalism.org, Bcorporation.net Holacracy.org and WorldBlu.com). Robert Putnam, political scientist, professor at Harvard University and author of *Bowling Alone: The Collapse and Revival of American Community* (2000), defines social capital as "connections among individuals – social networks and the norms of reciprocity and trustworthiness that arise from them" (p. 19).

The four prominent organizational approaches can be memorized using the acronym SALT:

SALT:
Sociocracy, Agile,
Lean Startup and Teal

SOCIOCRACY

The omnipresent movement, embracing all of this, is without doubt **sociocracy**, also called **dynamic governance**. Sociocracy consists of a few tools and principles and can be learned about online (see e.g. SociocracyForAll.org). It is also described in books such as *Many Voices One Song* (Rau and Koch-Gonzalez, 2018).

Sociocracy is a set of tools and principles that ensure shared power through self-governance, clarity, distributed leadership and feedback-rich environments.

The overarching virtues are **effectiveness** (the degree to which something is successful in producing a desired result) and **equivalence** (the condition of being equal).

As its governance is designed to be dynamic, the two key slogans for sociocratic governance are 'good enough for now' and 'safe enough to try', as these approaches allow for actions, interventions, flow and learning, instead of keeping things static.

Source: Rau and Koch-Gonzalez (2018, pp. 1-11).

Sociocracy – and its variant, holacracy (see Holacracy.org) – is based on the organizational component of 'the circle'. The organizational building blocks are circles of people, who work together and decide together. Holacracy is more descriptive and protocol oriented, whereas sociocracy is more pliable and approachable for the novice in this area.

The key elements of sociocracy are:

- The circle of employees with an aim, a domain and members
- How circles interact with each other through leadership and delegate roles, and how a general circle and mission circle tie everything together
- Meetings where all get to speak
- Decision-making through consent
- Structured feedback and learning mechanisms

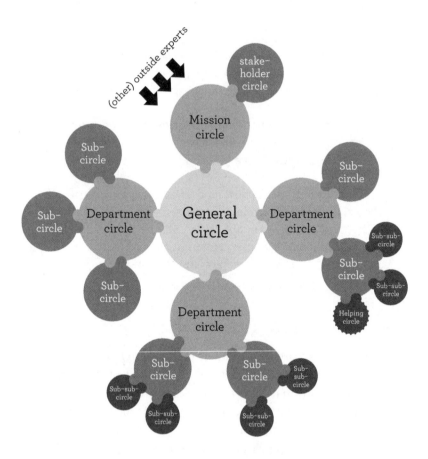

How the circles work together, in the double-linked style

Source: Rau and Koch-Gonzalez (2018)

Together, these elements and mechanisms address four areas of designing and running sociocratic teams (*Thrive-in Collaboration*, 2018):

Agility	Participation	Agreeing	Doing
Respond quickly and effectively to changing contexts	Build and maintain engagement and accountability	Tap into collective intelligence to create and evolve effective decisions	Do what needs to be done to create maximum value
• Clarify domains • Flow of information and influence • Link the domains • Structure the organization	• Focus on interactions • Contribute • Build collaboration • Learn and grow	• Clarify *why* • Co-create • Good-enough agreements • Experiment and learn	• Identify and distribute work • Prioritize backlogs • Pull in work • Review and improve

An overview of all principles and tools in sociocracy can be found online at Sociocracy30.org or in the book *Many Voices One Song* (Rau and Koch-Gonzalez, 2018):

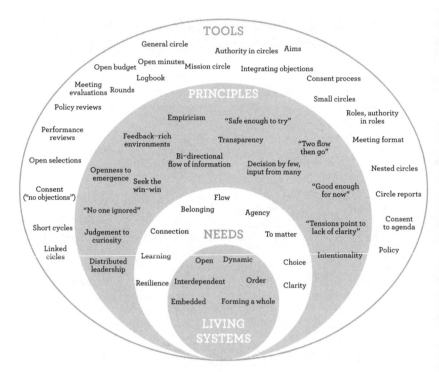

An overview of the tools, principles, needs and living systems on which sociocracy is built on.

Source: Rau and Koch-Gonzalez (2018)

The list of organizations that have embraced or tried out sociocratic operating systems is massive. Buurtzorg, Medium, Morningstar, Patagonia and Zappos are the most famous ones, having experimented with sociocracy and implemented all or some of it, with adjustments along the way.

AGILE

With the exponential development of technology in the 1970s, 1980s and 1990s, software programmers increasingly became frustrated with handling the changes required and managing the expectations of the users of their software.

They realized that expectations and reality changed between the point when a customer ordered or specified the software to the point when they received it. The programmers built what had been agreed, but the users' needs had changed in the meantime. Changes to specifications, updating documentation, testing and deployment became tedious activities that were always on the trailing edge of what users wanted.

In the late 1990s, a team of software developers and architects wanted to change this. Over a few years, they redesigned their approach to developing software and subsequently formulated the so-called *Agile Manifesto* (Agile Alliance, 2001):

> We are uncovering better ways of developing
> software by doing it and helping others do it.
> Through this work we have come to value:
>
> **Individuals and interactions**
> over processes and tools
> **Working software**
> over comprehensive documentation
> **Customer collaboration**
> over contract negotiation
> **Responding to change**
> over following a plan
>
> That is, while there is value in the items on
> the right, we value the items on the left more.
>
> Source: Agile Alliance (2001).

The members of the Agile Alliance were not the only people who wanted to change this. Methodologies such as eXtreme Programming (XP), Scrum, Scaled Agile Framework (SAFe), Crystal methodology and lean software development arose.

Over the past decade, Scrum has become the go-to methodology when it comes to discussing and applying agile software development. 'Agile' and 'Scrum' are even used interchangeably by some to simplify matters. However, whereas agile is a methodology, Scrum is a specific playbook (based on the agile methodology) with processes, protocols, roles and events. Jeff Sutherland's *Scrum: The Art of Doing Twice the Work in Half the Time* (2014) offers a valuable introduction to the framework along with case studies.

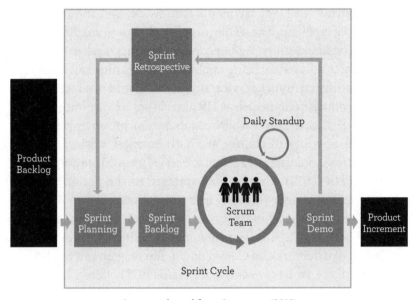

Source: Adapted from Scrum.org (2019)

Scrum.org (2019) describes Scrum's framework, values (courage, focus, commitment, respect and openness), roles (product owner, Scrum master, team and customer/user), process and events (sprint, sprint planning, daily scrum, sprint review and sprint retrospective) and artefacts (product backlog, sprint backlog, user stories and product increments).

Common to all of the methodologies above are high-frequent dialogue between user and developer, working in teams or pairs (not alone), building small increments of the business solution, and just-in-time decisions and changes. 'Inspect and adapt' is their maxim.

This mindset and methodology – implying dialogue, teamwork, small steps and change management – applies perfectly to the constantly changing business environment and new ways of working.

The application of agile thinking emerged and rooted itself firmly in IT departments worldwide, and the ripple effect of applying the agile mindset is now spreading to other business units. Agile processes, sprints, and daily or weekly standups are being applied in R&D units, sales and marketing, customer service, supply chain and production, and group functions such as HR and corporate communication – that is, in places where collaboration, group learning, and responding to change are both business critical and levers for employee engagement. Perry Timms' *Transformational HR* (2017) offers an introduction to the design and application of agile thinking in organizations.

Even so-called Enterprise Agile is being experimented with – that is, agility and incremental thinking from the board of directors and C-level down. Jim Hagemann Snabe and Mikael Trolle's *Dreams and Details* (2017) offers a vision of how to encourage business leaders to embrace this ambitious vision and enter more directly into execution and experimentation mode.

LEAN STARTUP

Highly related to agile thinking is the lean startup methodology. Whereas agile and Scrum use 'inspect and adapt', lean startup is built around the build–measure–learn feedback loop.

The approach is described by Eric Ries in his cornerstone book *The Lean Startup* (2011). Ries writes, "Rather than wasting time creating elaborate business plans, the Lean Startup offers entrepreneurs – in companies of all sizes – a way to test their vision continuously, to adapt and adjust before it is too late."

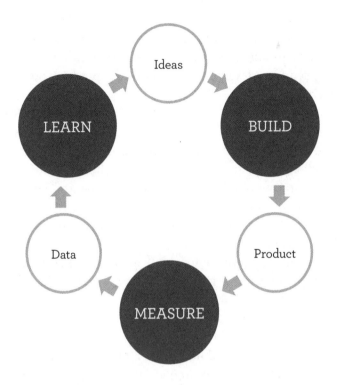

The development cycle for the lean startup.

Source: Ries (2011)

Ries describes the fundamentals of a successful start-up business:

1. Entrepreneurs are everywhere
2. Entrepreneurship is management
3. Validated learning
4. Innovation accounting
5. Build–measure–learn

A focus on what is known as the MVP (the minimal viable product) is key. However, equally important are (a) validated learning, where entrepreneurs frequently run experiments that test each element of the vision in order to learn how to build a sustainable business, and (b) the ability to pivot the product, process or organization, in a way that is designed to test a hypothesis about the product, business model or growth.

In his follow-up work *The Startup Way* (2017), Ries describes how the startup mentality and approach can be used inside corporate businesses to transform culture and drive long-term growth. This fits with the results of a scientific study by Lingfei Wu, Dashun Wang and James A. Ewans, who state that it is small teams that drive innovation and entrepreneurship forward in organizations (Wu, Wang and Ewans, 2019).

Decoding the inner mechanisms of small startups or scaleups and transferring that approach to corporate business is the core of Ries' work and fits very well with how exponential organizations are built.[1]

The Orange World described in this book is deliberately designed to foster and nurture teams and cultures where lean startup and entrepreneurial thinking are natural and encouraged.

THE BIRTH OF TEAL:
A CLASSIFICATION OF ORGANIZATIONS

In 2014, Frédéric Laloux published *Reinventing Organizations*, in which he codified a handful of characteristics of different organizations. Additionally, he provided motivation for abandoning the existing and dominant hierarchical structure and replacing it with something more living, self-governed and evolutionary. He introduced a simple and memorable colour code of five simplified ways to label culture, namely Red, Amber, Orange, Green and Teal. With that book, he provided a shared framework to relate to and the 'Teal Movement' was born.

Colour	Description	Guiding metaphor	Guiding metaphor	Current examples
Red	Constant exercise of power by chief to keep troops in line. Highly reactive, short-term focus. Thrives in chaotic environments.	Wolf pack	Division of labour Command authority	Organized crime Street gangs Tribal militias
Amber	Highly formal roles within a hierarchical pyramid. Top-down command and control. Future is a repetition of the past.	Army	Formal roles (stable and scalable hierarchies) Stable, replicable processes (long-term perspectives)	Catholic Church Military Most government organizations (public school systems, police departments)
Orange	Goal is to beat competition and to achieve profit and growth. Management by objectives (command and control over what, freedom over how).	Machine	Innovation Accountability Meritocracy	Multinational companies Investment banks Charter schools
Green	Focus on culture and empowerment to boost employee motivation. Stakeholders replace shareholders as primary purpose.	Family	Innovation Accountability Meritocracy	Businesses known for idealistic practices (e.g. Ben & Jerry's, Southwest Airlines, Starbucks, Zappos)
Teal	Self-management replaces hierarchical pyramid. Organizations are seen as living entities, oriented towards realizing their potential.	Living organism	Self-management Wholeness Evolutionary purpose	A few pioneering organizations

Source: Adapted from Laloux (2015)

Very quickly, this model became a go-to reference guide for debating the future of leadership and the future of work. Naturally, being a model, it is simplified and not an exhaustive description of organizations. But it provided – and still does – enough relevance and reflection for people to relate to and apply in their conversations.

Laloux describes three breakthroughs that characterize evolutionary Teal organizations:

Self-management: Teal Organizations have found the key to operate effectively, even at a large scale, with a system based on peer relationships, without the need for either hierarchy or consensus.

Wholeness: Organizations have always been places that encourage people to show up with a narrow 'professional' self and to check other parts of the self at the door. They often require us to show a masculine resolve, to display determination and strength, and to hide doubts and vulnerability. Rationality rules as king, while the emotional, intuitive, and spiritual parts of ourselves often feel unwelcome, out of place. Teal Organizations have developed a consistent set of practices that invite us to reclaim our inner wholeness and bring all of who we are to work.

Evolutionary purpose: Teal Organizations are seen as having a life and a sense of direction of their own. Instead of trying to predict and control the future, members of the organization are invited to listen in and understand what the organization wants to become, what purpose it wants to serve.

Source: Laloux (2014, p. 56).

Using this framework, I have made three observations. First, by far, most organizations are Orange. Second, the progressive organizations want to be more Teal. Third, in practice, every organization has elements of all colours.

USING TEAL AND ORANGE AS CATCH-ALL TERMS IN THIS BOOK

Reinventing Organizations established an updated language for old and new organizations. The term 'Orange' became the label for the existing corporate organizations, while the term 'Teal' became the label for the modern organization. Clearly, this was a simplification of the model (a simplification of a simplification), but, with those two colours in hand, a whole new kind of conversation could take place. And this is the same obviously naive (and obviously erroneous) approach we will use in this book:

This book uses 'Orange' as a catch-all term for organizational characteristics such as:	This book uses 'Teal' as a catch-all term for organizational characteristics such as:
Hierarchy and top-down structure	Self-governance
Governance and guidance	Principle-based collaboration
Management by objectives	Management by intent
Optimization for efficiency, efficacy and productivity	Optimization for impact and outcome
Provision of predictability	Wholeness
Provision of **alignment**	Provision of adaptability
	Provision of **autonomy**

The intent is to be able to create an update to the structure, a modern Orange World. This is a deliberate construction of opposites, and it serves its purpose as such:

to create a simple-to-understand, simple-to-apply tool for dialogue and reflection, both in management teams and in daily conversations in organizations. Laloux himself uses this construction, and in the back of his book is a full list of differences between the old and the modern world, or Orange and Teal.

I fully acknowledge the emergence and rightful application of Orange cultures, as they evolved out of a concrete need and created a replicable and scalable organizational model, able to deliver predictable services with predictable quality. Similarly to the emergence of Teal organizations, the spontaneous emergence of such self-governed structures was the result of an evolutionary development of collaboration requests, serving the need for adaptability in a constantly changing world.

Please also note that I do not categorize Orange with fear-based leadership or similar anxiety-infused wording, as I think it creates too much of a gap between the labels. Both Orange and Teal can create either safety or worries for leaders and employees, and I have met people with work-related stress from both worlds.

COMPARING WORLDS AND TERMINOLOGIES

Comparing the Orange and Teal labels to the manifesto of Responsive Org (see Responsive.org), we clearly find that the terms fit with the built-in opposites of the manifesto:

Characteristics of Orange	Characteristics of Teal
Profit	Purpose
Hierarchies	Networks
Controlling	Empowering
Planning	Experimentation
Privacy	Transparency

Comparing the Teal label to sociocracy (and holacracy), we again find striking similarities. The circles have the same characteristics as the Teal organization: self-governance, clear purpose and fairness.

And the same is true of agile and Scrum. Self-governed Scrum teams are very much Teal-esque, or sociocratic, based on principles of dialogue, collaboration, adaptability and interaction.

The old management styles	The new ways of working
Predictable Profit Hierarchies Controlling Planning Privacy	Adaptable Purpose Networks Empowering Experimentation Transparency
Hierarchy Command and control	*SALT:* Sociocracy and holacracy Agile and Scrum (and SAFe) Lean Startup Teal
Division of labour Best practices Fixed mindset	'Good enough for now' practices Growth mindset

Orange is a great fit for a predictable world. Teal is a great fit for an adaptable world. What we need is a combination of the two. What we need is an update to the business world: **a modern Orange World**.

TEAL DOTS IN AN ORANGE WORLD:

A MODEL FOR ORGANIZATIONAL THINKING

TAKING IDEOLOGY INTO REALITY

Is Teal realistic? Yes and no.

Teal (and similar movements such as holacracy) has been pedestalized as the holy grail of modern management. Once you go Teal, your organizational problems will be gone. Unicorns and rainbows will appear. However, this is clearly not the case. Laloux acknowledges this himself and advises readers not to oversimplify the model and the thinking.

I recall a full-day workshop in a flat organization with a progressive approach to new ways of working. Using the above-mentioned broad (and oversimplified) labelling, they characterized themselves as Teal... but during that workshop day they also identified situations, processes and activities that clearly belonged to the other colours.

In some areas they debated whether they were Orange – and even Red in a few heated moments. Sometimes they made decisions as if they were Green (family), and in other situations top-down in an Amber style. What they learned was that **Teal is a mindset and an intention**, a set of principles and mechanisms, and a framework for organizational identity, but with situational and contextual differences and deviations from the at times virtuous, puritan agreements that the employees make – and expect from each other. Reality is different from the ideal, and more mottled than the model.

Generally, two root causes are found here.

First, people are people, and interpersonal relationships can be tough and exhausting. We make mistakes, we get misaligned, we make promises without full-circle democratic alignment, etc. Conflicts are an unavoidable element of any organization, Teal or not. Constant dialogue and striving for mutual alignment and transparency are means to mitigate these challenges.

Second, such Teal-like cultures are hard to scale. When the team size grows beyond 12-15 employees, some challenges with staying updated and connected appear. Weekly meetings become long and seemingly uninteresting to all. Daily work happens in smaller groups and project teams. Subcultures begin to emerge. This leads to a lack of information, a lack of shared experiences and in some cases disconnection from the tribal feeling.

Several of the scaleup organizations I work with have reported similar challenges. Establishing a Teal feeling in a startup organization with fewer than 15 employees is doable (yet still hard). Conserving and nurturing it while scaling up to 50 or 200 employees is tremendously hard. Honestly, it's way easier to apply Orange to the organization, divide the employees into functional areas, create standard operating procedures and manage the organization using key performance indicators (KPIs) and objectives.

But this does not solve the problem of reinventing the organization to be suitable for a modern, changing world.

BALANCING ALIGNMENT AND AUTONOMY

The ultimate organizational goal is to have internal alignment between all activities, and (the right amount of) local autonomy in teams. We want the best of the Orange **alignment** and the best of the Teal **autonomy**.

Below is a categorization and description of how alignment and autonomy fit together, and what characterizes misalignment and lack of autonomy.

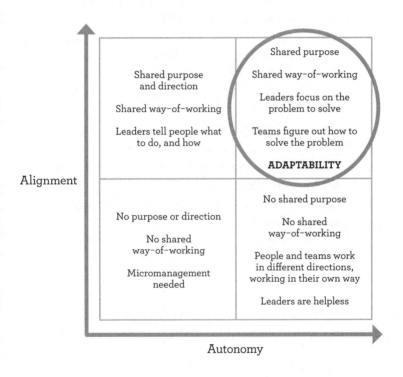

Source: Adapted from both Henrik Kniberg (2014) and Mark Richman (2014), this alignment/autonomy matrix illustrates the goal destination of the Teal Dots and the Orange World: a state where teams are autonomous and self-managed, working in alignment in an Orange World.

What we want to create is a mix or interplay between the predictability and scalability of the aligned Orange World, and the creativity and sustainability of the autonomous Teal teams.

Going forward, this book uses 'Teal' and 'Orange' as a new language for culture and mechanisms, and to describe new ways of working where the mindset is fundamentally different from the traditional approach of command and control. Once you understand the Teal/Orange nomenclature, you start seeing it all over the place:

- Teal teams in Orange organizations
- Teal organizations in Orange markets
- Teal mechanisms for committing to work in an Orange World of commands
- Teal KPIs in Orange KPIs
- Teal missions in an Orange mission
- Teal just-in-time planning/execution in an Orange waterfall prediction
- Teal leadership in an Orange management world
- Teal Dots in an Orange World

Teal is fitting for a startup. Pure Teal is not fitting for a scaleup, in most cases. Nor is Orange. And certainly not for a full-blown corporate entity. We need to find a new way of working that **augments** Orange with Teal.

Parts Two, Three and Four will help you do just that.

Unlearning is something some of
our colleagues struggle with,
as they are used to having guidelines and
standard operating procedures for everything.

We don't have that.
They have to think for themselves.

———

Thomas Gammelvind,
CEO, Trustworks A/S

Culture and fellowship

CHAPTER 3.
CASE STUDY: TRUSTWORKS
– A TEAL DOT IN AN ORANGE BUSINESS WORLD

Company characteristics	
Company name	**Trustworks A/S**
Industry	IT consulting, project management, business and solution architecture
Company size	Approximately 30 employees as of summer 2019 and growing steadily
Global presence	Copenhagen, Denmark
Teal Dots in an Orange World profile	Trustworks as a company is a full-blown Teal Dot in an otherwise Orange business world

Since the beginning in 2014, Trustworks has been a unique organization. Founded by four colleagues who broke out from Devoteam, a traditional multinational consulting service organization, Trustworks was designed fundamentally differently.

When I asked the CEO, Thomas Gammelvind, directly why, his immediate response was, "It had to be fun to go to work." He continued: "We were used to being measured on utilization and sales. We were tired of the hierarchy and decision-making structures. We wanted to build something that was based on relationships, knowledge, and personal growth."

Trustworks is different. Being present in a consultancy business, competition for customers and for talent is fierce. The good consultants are much sought after, and the customers are picky when it comes to whom they trust and engage with. In this Red Ocean,[2] Trustworks deliberately chose a different path, designing its own Blue Ocean: a Teal Dot in an otherwise Orange World.

MINDSET AND APPROACH

The overarching idea was to create an organization the founders wanted to be part of themselves. Being fed up with traditional Orange structures, they focused on self-governance, self-management and personal freedom. Crucial to their design was the idea of a flat organization, the culture, the relationships and absolutely as few processes as possible.

"Unlearning is something some of our colleagues struggle with," stated Gammelvind, "as they are used to having guidelines and standard operating procedures for everything. We don't have that. They have to think for themselves."

Over the following years, the company grew from four to over 15 colleagues, and in 2017 a Chief Culture Officer was hired, Michael Bruun Ellegaard. "Mindset and culture are way more important for us and for our hiring process," said Ellegaard. "We're looking for someone that fits in. Growth mindset is important, more than experience." This is also why all partners of Trustworks are active in the hiring interviews, and an intensive onboarding mechanism with a buddy programme is vital to the company's success. "Our colleagues must land properly. And the unlearning is vital to this," Gammelvind said.

"It is actually hard," one employee said, "to be part of something that is so undefined, to unlearn existing habits" – and several other employees said the same. Contrary to what is often deemed to be the case in the world of organizational development, this is especially hard for some of the younger employees. It can be hard to find your own role, and to understand what success looks like. They seek and need handles in a Teal world, with freedom, self-management, and anarchistic and rebellious colleagues. However, for the experienced employees, it is the other way around: "If the frame or guidance is not in place, I create it myself." That will not hold me back."

One employee described it as moving from the zoo to the savannah. In his old job, there were rules and structures, like the employees were in a cage in a zoo. "Here," he stated, "I'm set free on the savannah. There are no rules. It was like an illusion at first. Is there something I'm missing? Something I don't see? But it turned out that it felt great."

Source: From a company event at Trustworks, where the employees give feedback. In the middle in the white shirt: Thomas Gammelvind, CEO.

The relationships, the nearly family-like approach and the humanistic design were emphasized multiple times in the interviews I conducted with both leaders and employees at Trustworks. Small teams, no hierarchy, and honest and genuine interest in each other are the central points of the company's culture.

The mindset of self-governance permeates everything at Trustworks. What would you do? How and where do you create the most and best value? What is in our best and mutual interest? These areas are what the employees' success and performance are evaluated against. They must share the DNA of the company and contribute to the success of the team. Being a consultant with high utilization and creating high revenue is not enough.

A fantastic example of self-management and autonomy is the freedom to give feedback on tasks and activities to customers. If an employee does not want to take the responsibility for a customer or a project assignment, they are free to highlight this in order to avoid similar activities going forward.

Trustworks does not have a detailed company handbook with rules and processes written in it. Instead, employees are encouraged to think for themselves, or to ask a colleague, for example on Slack. "If you ask a question, people take the time to answer, including when they are located with a customer. When you post a question, you have a handful of useful comments within a few hours. This is a part of our DNA. We are here for each other," an employee said.

Source: From a collaboration training session at Trustworks.
To the left in the white shirt, Michael Bruun Ellegaard, Chief Culture Officer.

MECHANISMS AND TOOLING

What follows is a list of mechanisms that Trustworks uses to run its organization.

Organizational design: CEO, a leadership team of four partners and a Chief Culture Officer. Approximately 30 employees, all with a reference point to the CEO, Gammelvind.

Organizational rhythm: Weekly Friday-morning meeting, where everybody meets for information-sharing, updating the company Kanban board and professional sparring.

Personal relationships: Annually, every employee has a 'key purpose conversation' (KPC) with the Chief Culture Officer, Ellegaard, which is supported by frequent 'touchbase' meetings. Both Gammelvind and Ellegaard underline that this is not a classic regular performance appraisal or wellbeing conversation. It revolves around mindset, culture and alignment with the overall purpose of Trustworks.

Professional mentoring: In addition to the KPC, more formalized professional sparring and mentoring conversations take place between each employee and someone from the partner team. The purpose is to ensure continuous development and engagement within the domain areas and ensure personal and professional development as consultants and advisors. The sparring sessions take place at a frequency that fits with the individual's need regarding tooling, tasks, behaviour, etc.

Cultural Cocktails: To have a different kind of dialogue, the Chief Culture Officer Ellegaard has initiated Cultural Cocktails where he serves drinks to a smaller group of employees to create a more informal setting for feedback and reflection.

Knowledge-sharing: Trustworks' so-called 'bubbles' (online and offline communities of practice) are created if someone sees the need for one. They can be in professional areas, such as CRM (customer relationship management) systems or organizational change management, or in industry domains, such as finance or engineering.

Communication: An internal social media platform (in this instance, Slack) is the company's main communication tool. Emails are primarily used for external communication. This is very much a part of the unlearning process, as most employees are used to heavy email cultures. Bi-weekly, Gammelvind records a ten-minute 'state of the nation' video to share with the whole organization. The opening rate of the video is above 80%. "People watch it or listen to it when they have time for it, for example on the train to work," Ellegaard commented.

Automation and augmented leadership: Some home-built software tools support the management and the employees in making sure that they are on top of their agreements. A plug-in to Slack (with the tongue-in-cheek name HAL9000) nudges everybody to fill in their time sheets daily and follows up if they are behind. Likewise, a tool named MU/TH/ER (read: mother) keeps an eye on allocation rates and distribution, to the benefit of both leadership and employees.

Salary: This consists of a fixed monthly payment. There are no performance reviews or bonus targets, either personally or for the organization, but 10% of the annual revenue is split between all employees in alignment with their individual monthly salaries.

Organizational learning: Annually, $750 (€670) per employee is pooled for shared learning activities, for example key notes, courses or training activities in-house.

Personal education: Each employee has an annual budget on $4,500 (€4,000) to invest in education, at their own discretion.

IT budget: Each employee has a bi-annual budget of $3,700 (€3,300) to invest in hardware, at their own discretion.

RESULTS AND THE FUTURE

Clearly, this works and shows concrete results.

Trustworks had a revenue of $4.9 million (€4.4 million) in their fiscal year 2018/2019 with a profit of nearly $1.19 million (€1.08 million), with continuous growth. They have grown to approximately 30 employees and earned their second consecutive *Børsen* Gazelle in 2019 (the Gazelle award was established by the Danish financial paper *Børsen* and is given to organizations that – among other things – for over four consecutive years have continuous growth and have at least doubled their revenue in that period).

"Growth," both Gammelvind and Ellegaard said, "is only possible if we keep focusing on culture." The tough part is to find time to establish and nurture relationships and interpersonal connections to the culture, when the growth rate is high. At some point, the culture may break into smaller or larger fragments.

They continue: "Role models and cultural adhesiveness are vital for us, to solve the new challenges that arise when we grow. For example, handling a Friday meeting with more than 50 employees where the individual employee feels connected and the meeting is valuable – or handling career development in a flat hierarchy." It takes constant investment and energy to maintain that kind of dynamic stability.

From Trustworks' culture and mechanisms, it is clear to see that it is a Teal Dot in an Orange World. Its Blue Ocean is not based on its products and services – its *what* – but on its identity and organizational culture – its *how*.

YOUR LEADERSHIP PROFILE:

A MATURITY ASSESSMENT

Before you read any further, it's important to ask yourself the following questions: What kind of leadership profile do you have? What kind of organizational culture do you have?

This Maturity Assessment maps habits and behaviour in six areas and thereby provides an understanding of leadership style. It uses the five organizational development stages described by Frédéric Laloux in *Reinventing Organizations* (2014) as a starting point.

The result of the analysis should be a conversation starter, allowing you to evaluate your current leadership style and initiate your organization's transformation so that it will be fit for the future.

The Maturity Assessment was developed by Puk Falkenberg as part of her thesis *Knowledge Creation in a Knowledge-Intensive Firm: How to Conceptualize Tacit Knowledge in a Change Management SME* at the University of Southern Denmark, in collaboration with leaders and managers from a number of large Danish companies (Falkenberg, 2016). In 2018 it was expanded to embrace modern organizational change management.

First, decide on the organizational scope for your self-assessment. Are you investigating your team, your department or your organization? The term 'unit' is used below as an umbrella for the team, department or organizational scope you choose.

Second, below you will find five groups of three questions, all with five options for answers. Circle the answer that fits your behaviour the best.

Finally, you should reflect on the results.

PURPOSE AND DIRECTION

Question	Red	Amber
Do the employees know what problem the team solves, and for whom?	The management tells the employees what to do, from case to case.	Yes, the unit has a strong tradition of solving a specific set of problems and has a set way of doing it.
How do your unit's purpose and direction evolve?	The right amount of purpose and direction are given to the employees from case to case.	The unit have had the same purpose for a long time.
How transparent is the unit with regards to results, targets, investments and profit?	The management decides that, from case to case.	It's on a need-to-know basis, documented in the processes

INNOVATION

Question	Red	Amber
Why and when are the employees innovative?	Because management asks them to be.	It's not the top focus, because there are stable, replicable processes that employees adhere to.
Who is responsible for being creative and innovative in your organization?	Management initiates the activities and appoints a team for it.	Management initiates the activities and decides on the team, according to the guidelines and procedures.
How does the unit handle mistakes?	Mistakes will be punished.	The employees make sure not to make mistakes by following the processes.

Orange	Green	Teal
Yes, the unit has a set of objectives that employees work towards. We do that to be better than our competition.	Yes, the unit solves our stakeholders' problems as well as our shareholders'.	Yes, the unit solves problems for the customers and the community (and maybe even for society).
The top management adjusts the purpose and direction from time to time, based on the forces of the market and our competitors' actions.	The purpose and direction evolve to serve the need of the stakeholders.	Everybody in the unit is part of formulating the purpose, and can adjust the direction themselves, all the time.
All employees are on a regular basis informed of the status of the KPIs and the financials.	All employees have reasonable insight into both input/output and financials.	We are transparent with everything, except personal and legal issues.

Orange	Green	Teal
To beat competition.	Because it's their passion.	Because it benefits the customers and is a way to solve problems – and it's fun and valuable.
A dedicated department is responsible for innovation, research and development.	The ones who have the skills and drive – and the stakeholders are involved.	Anybody can be responsible for being innovative and creative. The customers, the community – and even our competitors from time to time – are involved.
Mistakes hinder the growth and development of the unit, so activities are closely monitored to avoid mistakes.	The unit talk about the mistakes and are forgiving, but they hate mistakes.	The unit embrace mistakes and learn from them. This is a part of evolving.

CULTURE

Question	Red	Amber
Who is responsible for each employee's wellbeing and development?	The management decides what skills are needed and how the employees should develop.	Employees can see from the guidelines what's required in order to develop and advance. Wellbeing comes naturally from the stability of the structure. Employees know what's expected from them.
What is the manager's role?	To distribute tasks and make decisions.	To send tasks and decisions to the right level, according to the guidelines.
Who makes the decisions, and how?	The manager, by telling the employees how they want things done.	The decisions are taken at the right level and according to the guidelines. If there is any doubt, things are escalated.

Orange	Green	Teal
It's a split between the employee and the manager. There is a regular process where employee performance is evaluated and a development plan is designed. Likewise, wellbeing is measured regularly.	The unit see themselves as a family and they have joint responsibility for each other, regarding both development and wellbeing. They have strong social values and everybody is treated with fairness.	The employee is responsible – but we coach each other all the time. Self-management is expected, and development is discussed together constantly. Wellbeing is discussed weekly, even daily.
To ensure that employees focus on the objectives and push their performance to the max.	To ensure a great culture.	To enable engagement and traction.
The level of decision-making power is agreed with the manager. Only rarely are things escalated, in order not to lose control.	Decisions are made as a unit. Members of the unit listen to each other, and often they want to agree before moving forward.	Anybody can make decisions on anything, but they must seek advice to understand the impact of their decisions.

ORGANIZING AND DELIVERY

Question	Red	Amber
How do employees collaborate?	The unit has very small sub-teams, and sometimes employees work on their own.	The unit collaborates in the teams, based on specific, predefined roles as described in the guidelines and processes.
How are tasks delegated? How do employees commit to tasks?	Management handles that, so employees don't have to think about it.	Mostly it's documented in the guidelines and processes. Employees commit to tasks that are described in their specific, predefined role.
Who tells the employees how to do their job?	The manager. They have a clear expectation on how to do the job.	It is documented in the guidelines and processes. Each employee is trained and clearly knows how to do the work.

Orange	Green	Teal
The unit collaborates mostly within the teams but also across the organization. Collaboration is focused on the objectives.	The unit collaborates as a family.	The unit collaborates freely across boundaries and structures. Employees decide on the roles, and they shift from time to time. We are also networked with the community – and even our competitors from time to time.
The unit mostly agree on the level of delegation from task to task, to ensure employee commitment.	The unit agree on delegation and commitment as a group, jointly. The unit are empowered to make decisions on the delegation too.	The unit are self-managed. They debate and adjust the delegation setup frequently and redistribute the tasks if needed. Individuals oversee their own commitment. They can propose a change to the task, so that they have higher willingness to commitment.
The employees can decide themselves, and we have several best-practice approaches to lean into.	The unit agree together on how to do it.	Employees can decide and then interact with colleagues and customers to openly and frequently calibrate the approach.

ORGANIZATIONAL CHANGE MANAGEMENT

Question	Red	Amber
How does the company practice change management?	Management reacts to change and tells employees how to respond. Changes are only made when necessary and out of crisis.	Management creates a so-called 'burning platform' for changing. Actions are typically reactive instead of proactive.
How does management handle internal change? How do the employees react?	Only management can initiate internal change. Employees are only involved when needed. Management decides from case to case.	Internal change seldom happens and is only considered by management when procedure fails.
How does the company react to external change both positive and negative?	Mostly management reacts out of fear and tries to control external change. Management decides from a command-and-control perspective.	External change is only considered when it is required of the company to change procedures – or when losing market to the competition (for example).

REFLECTION

Where is your organizational gravitation point? Towards Orange or Teal?

Are some of the areas out of balance with the rest?

Would your leadership peers answer in the same way?

Orange	Green	Teal
A special unit or appointed change agents manage the change project step by step. The unit communicate and inform employees about the change, and measure how change initiatives engage and impact the project.	Every stakeholder is involved in every step of the change process. Everyone takes an active part and is involved in big (and small) change decisions.	Change is an organizational capability where every employee reacts according to the purpose and the specific context. Navigating change is something we just do.
Change can be suggested to the change unit if there is likely to be a return on investment. Management approves when a business case has been reviewed.	Employees can suggest changes and can counsel each other and stakeholders on a given internal change.	Anyone can take the lead on a given change – big or small.
To beat the competition, gain a new market, react to politics or the like. Changes are only acted upon when there is security about a positive outcome.	The company unites around a given external threat (or possibility) and decides on the direction to take regarding the change affecting the company.	The organizational capability to navigate change is a strength that helps it to foresee and be proactive (as well as fast) when external change hits.

What would the result be if you changed organizational scope, whether by zooming in on a smaller part of the unit, zooming out to a broader scope or looking at cross-organizational collaboration?

Should you change something? What would the outcome be? How urgent is it?

PART TWO:
NEW WAYS
OF WORKING

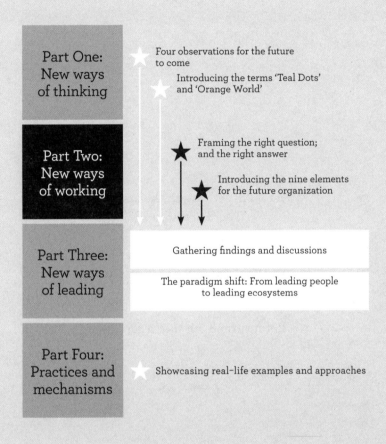

This part challenges a popular approach to modern grand-scale organizations and instead formulates the right question and answer to be investigated in order to design modern, progressive organizations that are scalable and adaptable. It introduces the nine elements that go into building modern organizations for the future.

Here, I'm set free on the savannah.
There are no rules.

It was like an illusion at first.
Is there something I'm missing?
Something I don't see?

But it turned out that it felt great.

———

Employee,
Trustworks A/S

**Self-managed
delivery teams**

CHAPTER 4.

THE ILLUSION OF CORPORATE COLLABORATION

Way too many leaders who I meet have the illusion that their organization is unified in working towards a shared goal. They use narratives such as, "We work like gears and cogs in a well-oiled machine, where everyone matters and contributes to the same goal," and they take pride in sharing that narrative with their C-level peers. However, the truth is that the employees rarely work together in that clock-like manner. More likely, they work in parallel, beside each other.

There appears to be a disconnection between the C-level and the rest of the organization about how work and collaboration is described, designed and executed. Corporate collaboration is often just an illusion. Instead, corporate co-working is the norm, based on process optimization, division of labour and functional specialization.

We need to change that because – as described in the previous chapters – this kind of production framework is fitting for a business world that expects the same tomorrow as it gets today. Most of the businesses I encounter are good at delivering what they did yesterday, just better, faster and cheaper. However, new problems and opportunities arise in the wake of technological and societal developments. The illusion of corporate collaboration is one of the impediments we are facing, making it hard or impossible to design and embrace new solutions.

Let's burst the bubble of so-called corporate collaboration. To me, it's often nothing more than a mirage.

NEW WAYS OF WORKING: "WE DON'T DO THAT – WE'RE TOO BUSY IMPROVING"

Imagine you are part of a classic corporate organization. It might have 50 employees, 200, 1,000 or 10,000. Once you start forming teams (in plural), departments and business units, the mechanisms are the same despite the size.

Business is good. Revenue is growing. So is the stock price. There is a continuous 2%, 3%, 5% increase each year. Maybe even with double-digit growth. Most of your organizational focus is on two things: continuous improvements and customer service. You invest significantly in projects and programmes that can eliminate waste, increase productivity and ensure that you are doing things right. In other words, you are good at doing what you did yesterday, just better, faster and cheaper. This is just like what was described as Orange in the previous chapters.

Most of the top and middle managers in these settings know and understand that a paradigm shift in the business world is emerging and emerging rapidly. They read and hear about technological advancements, changes in society, and new requirements from customers and employees. They go to networking meetings to hear about the future of work and the new organizational styles, and they debate these ideas in their coffee meetings with each other.

Often, I hear three things (paraphrasing):

"This Teal [or agile or Scrum or lean startup] thing is really interesting, and I really like it! I recall when I was in such a team once. It was both fun and productive. But it will never happen at our place, on a large scale. We cannot transform the whole company to work this way."

"It might fit in those vibrant and innovative areas where people are creative. It will never work with us. We do a lot of 'run the business', have blue-collar workers and have

*standard operating procedures. Teal is not applicable at our
business unit."*

*"In our management meetings and in our strategy ses-
sions we never discuss this. It is seen and mentioned as some
kind of joke or utopia. We briefly air the thought, conclude
that it will never happen here, and then someone says: 'Let's
get back to business.' If anything happens at all, it's something like a three-month focus on empowerment, rolled out
through internal communication, and then nothing more."*

Partly they are right. Partly they are wrong.

Transforming a 10,000-employee corporate into a Teal
setup is nearly impossible. Very few have done it. Haier
Group is one of the few, and it takes tremendous effort,
time and money (Corporate Rebels, 30 January 2019).

The solution we're looking for is not to turn everything
into Teal Dots, or circles of circles, as were introduced in
the section in Chapter 2 about sociocracy. Instead, **the
solution is to create an Orange World on which the Teal
Dots can emerge, live, grow and evaporate when their
aim has been met.**

Change the mindset. Change the approach to innovation. Change the cultural traits and virtues. Change the
leadership mechanisms and roles. And then, change your
organization from using ingrown hierarchical thinking to
systemic platform thinking.

This is the solution: create an Orange World with
Teal Dots.

THE CHALLENGE OF GROWTH:
LEADERSHIP BANDWIDTH

Organizational growth has an intrinsic challenge. As soon as a company grows to a size where teams start to be more independent, it needs mechanisms to help the teams be both aligned and autonomous and have access to both support and colleagues.

This means that the manager – or the management team – cannot be everywhere in the organization to constantly support, serve and supply the employees with advice, sparring and clear prioritization. **The leadership bandwidth for dialogue and interactions becomes the scarcest resource.** This is a very natural behaviour in any organization; tasks that require the management's focus will limit their time and ability to nurture and maintain relationships with the other parts of the organization. The social capital is drawn to the magnetic anchor points of the projects and activities and is no longer uniformly distributed.

The classic, best-practice reaction is then to slowly – but irrevocably – introduce reporting structures between teams, steering committees, project management offices, portfolio review sessions, KPIs, yearly employee development processes, performance reviews and so on. This leads to bureaucracy. It leads to the old Orange bureaucracy.

The way the local team managers and project managers behave and act is a result of the bureaucratic premise and culture they are part of. They optimize their team activities to fit with the surroundings. For some, this leads to micro-management, command and control, and what seemingly is a copy of Orange. For others, this leads to the opposite: they establish Teal-like teams. Of course, team leaders themselves play a part in the cultures of teams, but the organizational culture and stakeholder landscape affect the team culture to a much larger degree: **the construct**

and thinking in the bureaucratic fabric heavily influence the emergent culture in the teams, as the team culture is a result of the organizational culture, the team leadership and the team members themselves.

If the organization as a whole is designed and run as a well-oiled machine, chances are that the team leads will replicate that approach, as the management style and thinking trickle down from the board of directors to the C-level to the executive layers to middle managers and then to team leads – and finally to the employees. This creates predictability and optimization. This creates the bureaucracy, which in turn leads to local, functional, silo-like teams and business units. This is Orange organization and culture with Orange teams.

But, if the organizational mindset is one of adaptability, the culture and bureaucratic mechanisms are not designed and rolled out from the top. Such ideas emerge out of need for clarity and learning, not for optimization alone. Now, according to the prevalent literature on modern workplaces, structures such as SALT (see Chapter 2) are the modern, epiphany-like and seemingly correct response to that.

This seems to be possible in discrete, isolated situations, where the organization is of a limited size (under approximately 50 employees) and the idea of Teal is built into the foundation of the company, but a full-blown roll-out of Teal (e.g. **transforming** a bank with 1,000 employees) is not something I see happen. Instead, let's observe the existing mechanisms of actual working conditions in Orange organizations, where Teal teams and business units emerge.

THE POWER OF SMALL TEAMS
IN THE CORPORATE WORLD

One idea that is getting more and more support is the notion of the power of small teams.

For example, in the mid-2000s I was one of two project managers heading a large IT project at Novo Nordisk, a world-leading pharmaceutical company in Denmark. At that time the company consisted of just under 30,000 employees across the globe. We worked on the project for two years, from the idea of rebuilding the global intranet to go-live after year one and initiating the migration of local solutions to a central platform with access for all after year two. During that period, we dynamically shaped the team from four to 25 employees and vendor consultants, and it all took place in small teams. A project management team. A platform and infrastructure team. A design and user experience team. An organizational change management and communication team. A migration team. All those teams contained five to seven people at the maximum, worked with a clear aim and independence, and with daily and weekly check-ins in our project room. None of us had the full picture of the plan, the solution or the challenges, but together we solved the issues as they arose. We were a small and evolutionary team of teams, not a fixed functional form.

This is not an isolated example. Many executives I have spoken with have recalled similar situations. Small teams get things done. Small teams identify the breakthroughs and come up with innovations. Small teams, even on the C-level, handle the vital strategic activities. Small teams make the mergers and acquisitions work. It's always small teams that stand out from the organizational fabric.

Getting extraordinary things done in the modern corporate world happens in small teams only, not in large operational structures. This observation is unrelated to the size and impact of the organization. Success is not an attribute of corporate collaboration but of small, self-managed teams in a team-of-teams structure.

> ### Teal Dots observation number 1:
>
> Getting extraordinary things done in the modern corporate world happens in small teams only

This is both a reaction to the stiffness of the corporate world and a view into a world to come. Over the past decades, functional organizational structures have emerged, with division of labour, specialized business units and a focus on optimization for productivity. In their paper "Large Teams Develop and Small Teams Disrupt Science and Technology", Lingfei Wu, Dashun Wang and James A. Ewans (2019) give us an understanding of why this happens. They write:

> *Increases in team size have been attributed to the specialization of scientific activities, improvements in communication technology, or the complexity of modern problems that require interdisciplinary solutions. ... Observed differences between small and large teams are magnified for higher-impact work, with small teams known for disruptive work and large teams for developing work. ... Smaller teams have tended to disrupt science and technology with new ideas and opportunities, whereas larger teams have tended to develop existing ones. ... Work from larger teams builds on more recent and popular developments, and attention to their work comes immediately. By contrast, contributions by*

smaller teams search more deeply into the past, are viewed as disruptive to science and technology and succeed further into the future – if at all. (p. 1-2)

As to why this works, Wu (2019) states:

*Experimental and observational research on groups reveals that individuals in large groups think and act differently – they generate fewer ideas, recall less learned information, reject external perspectives more often and tend to neutralize each other's viewpoints. ... **Small and large teams are different in nature. Small teams ask questions and disrupt existing theories. Large teams answer questions and stabilize established paradigms.***

In *The Innovator's Dilemma* (1997), Clayton Christensen, an author and academic at Harvard University, similarly argues that functional, corporate constructs are made for polishing and refining products and processes. The corporates are made for running the business. Changes and innovations happen when you break this structure. Small, cross-skilled teams are capable of this – not large, functional teams.

"But," the executives quickly interject after recalling the power and agility of the small teams, "it could not happen without them knowing who to contact in the organization." True. Another observation related to observation number 1 is that small teams work on a fabric of support.

The success of the Teal teams relies on two factors:
1. Having a fabric, a world to live in. The Teal Dots have basic needs to be in place: corporate functions such as purchasing, people and culture, legal, and IT. They need funding and sponsorship, and they need someone to give them sparring and remove impediments, when appropriate. They need some amount of Orange.

2. Having a strong and active ecosystem and network (both internally and externally) containing subject matter experts, corporate change agents, influencers and door-openers.

This is a key point in the design of the new ways of working, and it is where the purity of the somewhat theoretical, overdesigned and evangelistic progressive models falls short.

It's not pure Teal or sociocracy.
It's not pure Orange either.
It's not functional hierarchy only.
It's not full flat organization either.

It's a mix.
It's a networked, modern Orange World with networked Teal Dots and networked humans.
It's an ecosystem.

It's complex. And it has a complex but not complicated solution.

RETHINKING
THE PROBLEM

THE CHALLENGE OF MODERN ORGANIZATIONS: ASKING THE WRONG QUESTION

Many top and middle managers have seen the challenge before them: they need to change their organizational modus operandi to something that is adaptable, resilient, innovative and attractive to talent. They recognize the push of the inevitable transformation and the pull from the seemingly greener pastures of new ways of working. They understand how SALT (sociocracy, agile, lean startup and Teal) works. And they might have heard the success stories of Menlo, WD-40 and Widen, to mention a few.

And then they sigh, shake their heads and give up. They ask: "How on Earth can we do that? How can we implement something like that as an organization? We are never going to be able to embrace SALT! It is a massive, massive change, and I don't see that happening any time soon. Plus, we have our board of directors meeting coming up, and we're behind our sales budget. I cannot see Teal happening at all."

And then they return to their normal, efficient, predictable way of working.

Their mistake is that they asked the **wrong questions**.

The direct response to the managers' questions and reactions is: "You're right! It cannot be done. You are never going to transform your organization to a fully fledged Teal organization, or Enterprise Agile. A few can, though, but that is extremely hard. Leave that thought in peace."

The right questions:

How might we create an organization that
is aligned, autonomous and adaptable?

How might we design our organization so that
it is resilient to change and human centric,
and in such a way that we can handle the
transformation in a manageable way
as part of our daily life?

How might we create something where every
employee experiences a Teal or agile-like culture,
with mechanisms that are truly scalable?

From my experiences over the past decades, working
with modern organizations, transformational leadership
and progressive thinkers, the right answer is to create
Teal Dots, redesign the space between the Teal Dots,
redesign the modern Orange World, and establish a
hyper-connected network between the organizational
gravitational points.

Create a modern Orange World for Teal Dots.

THE RIGHT SOLUTION: DESIGNING A DYNAMIC SOLUTION TO A DYNAMIC PROBLEM

The advancements that are happening in technology and sociology call for new ways of working.

We should exploit the technological leaps in both our production and our delivery mechanisms, in order to support our teams and employees, distribute work and activities, provide clarity and transparency, and augment our leadership and coaching skills.

A new wave of employees with digital affinity seek organizations that have the same characteristics as Teal/sociocratic teams: clear aim, direction, efficiency, equivalence and freedom (Krautwald, 2018). Humanism has made a massive footprint in the area of leadership, and intelligence quotients (IQ), emotional quotients (EQ), network quotients (NQ) (Bøtter, 2012) and meaningfulness quotients (MQ) (Albæk, 2018) are being debated on the C-level and in HR circles.

Sustainable leadership is omnipresent, with a balanced focus on planet, purpose, people and profit. In a constantly shifting business world:

- We need to stay relevant to our employees
- We need to stay relevant to our customers
- We need to balance run-the-business with grow-the-business
- We need to focus on impact and outcome
- We need to take care of the planet, the people and the profit
- We need a balanced approach to risk-taking

The approaches that are emerging are far more humanistic than mechanistic. Teal and sociocracy are fantastic examples of this that are designed around the need for distributed leadership and distributed decision-making, the willingness to create engagement, the need for impact and achievements, and personal development. They work but are hard to implement and scale in organizations above 50 employees, let alone a bank with 10,000 global employees.

What we need is a balanced approach – one that is scalable, sustainable, impactful and profitable. One that expects the unexpected and can react accordingly.

The solution must solve these requests:

- Able to support Teal Dots – that is, self-managed delivery teams
- Able to make tactical changes fast enough
- Able to distribute tasks to the right places
- Able to distribute decision-making to the right places
- Able to support dialogue across Teal Dots
- Able to create impact
- Able to create profit

The goal is to create an organizational design that is sustainable and resilient in an ever-changing world, and at the same time be applicable to organizations from 50 to 5,000 employees.

THE WRONG SOLUTION:

The wrong solution to the challenge would be to apply the old tools as we know them: form a task force, execute an investigation to analyse the problem, design and engineer a solution, and put it into production. Then, create a functional structure and KPIs, follow-up mechanisms, and spreadsheets for reports and monitoring – and maybe even have a standard operating procedure with best practices in it.

This is an 'if [this] then [that]' approach, based on the premise that we know, understand and can intelligently analyse the situation, as we were taught in school and have practised in the business world for decades. 'All things being equal' thinking does not apply here. We need to solve new problems with new tools.

The right solution:

Abandon the idea of teams working in hierarchy. Instead, consider the idea of several self-managed teams with their own aims, domains, members, ecosystems, rhythms and responsibilities. Apply Teal or sociocratic thinking to these circles or Teal Dots. Teal Dots should be small, with a maximum of five to seven employees.

Create an ecosystem. Redesign the organizational support system to be one that acts as a platform that the Teal Dots spawn on, live on and evaporate from. This is your modern Orange World: a platform-way-of-working or organization-as-a-service to the Teal Dots. The organization serves the teams, not the other way around.

Teal Dots can work together as circles with neighbouring circles, in small Teal ecosystems. They might resemble flowers, with petals surrounding a central circle. The Teal flowers should be limited to, say, a maximum of five to seven Teal Dots.

Create a rhythm of frequent touchpoints for
dialogue between the Teal Dots and the Teal
flowers. Form advisory boards to each Teal flower,
not for reporting but for support.

Nurture the internal network between employees
who are subject matter experts, information brokers
or social anchor points. Use it for feedback loops,
for idea generation, for dialogue, and for access
to experts and expertise. You might form
professional communities of practice too.

Make sure that the group's functions are proactive,
are part of the rhythm and take an interest
in the touchpoints.

Expect the unexpected. Provoke the unexpected.
Use your rhythm to react.

Develop your mindset, mechanisms and
structure at the same time.

Create humane and sustainable leadership,
based on connectedness.

THE RAKE AND THE FLOWER

Ask any leader to draw their organization, and they draw a functional hierarchy. Without hesitation, they start from the top of the paper, then draw the CEO, the C-level managers and the middle managers, and finally, at the bottom, they draw boxes with team names on them. It never fails. And it is always an illusion.

This functional hierarchy, which I will refer to as 'the rake' due to the visual similarity, emerged from the idea of the division of labour, where an organization's work is split into specialized areas so employees can focus on a few tasks, a few touchpoints and a few skills, so that they can optimize the organizational effort to maximize the output.

However, the following five characteristics kick in as soon as an organization grows to have more than about 20 employees.

First, hierarchy is great for predictability but not for adaptability. See, for example, the characteristics that Responsive Org describes very well in its manifesto (see Responsive.org). However, predictability is not always the desired trait, especially in a world that calls for adaptability (Deloitte, 2017).

Second, an increasing amount of work requires cross-functional skills and effort, meaning that the actual work does not take place in functional departments but in collaboration across teams, departments, business units and even outside the company's perimeter.

Third, leaders have come to understand that value streams are best for providing the impact that customers want and creating value for customers. This means that modifications (or 'mutants' or 'bastards' as some call them) of the hierarchy have evolved, for example the matrix organization or the project organization.

Fourth, innovative breakthroughs appear in small, cross-functional teams (Wu, Wang and Ewans, 2019).

Lastly, groups split into subgroups. Cultures split into subcultures. It happens as soon as the organization is larger than a handful of employees. The effort needed to maintain rapport and connection with everyone, in each individually preferred way, grows exponentially with the addition of each member, and is soon impossible to handle. Subgroups and subcultures form rapidly and are shaped by those individuals who have the social capital. In fortunate situations, social capital and production responsibility are shared among the same employees, but this is not always the case, as shown in numerous analyses of organizational networks (see later in this book).

The real work takes place in circles, or circles of circles, as correctly modelled in sociocracy. Employees work together in a project or in a service or maintenance department, collaborate and co-ordinate with each other, and may have a single or a few points of contact with the colleagues or customers to whom they provide help. This is unrelated to the maturity of the organization; however, the more progressive and modern the organization is, the more self-governance appears in the circles. This happens either by delegation and support from the management and culture or by rebellion and autonomy in the team and from the team members. These are the Teal Dots, and they work together in Teal flower-like ecosystems.

The new way of working is to create a culture in which these Teal Dots and ecosystems can emerge and appear (either initiated by the management or emerging spontaneously from the employees), live and thrive, and dissolve when their work is done. **Your task as a modern leader is to create this environment – create this modern Orange World in which Teal Dots exist.**

Once you have understood the dynamics of sociocratic mechanisms and experienced how they work in real life, you will soon realize that the drawing of the circles and their interactions is to a large extent topologically the same as drawing a hierarchy. "The hierarchy is just seen and drawn from above. The circles and the hierarchy are the same," one leader shared with me, whispering, like he had revealed a secret of the sociocratic world that no one talks about. "It's the emperor's new clothes," he added, referring to the famous short story by the Danish author Hans Christian Andersen.

What is missing in the drawing and in the model of the real-life embrace of the SALT models is the **network**, which weaves it all together.

Teal Dots observation number 2:

Work happens in highly connected networks

In 2015, Jacob Morgan described the future organization as a mixture of a hierarchy and flat parts, namely the 'flatarchy'. In 2017, Deloitte named their prediction 'network of teams', and the evidence shows that their foresight of the future organization was correct. The challenge is to create this network on the platform – to create the networked Orange World for the teams and the network to live in.

How things were

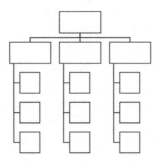

How things work

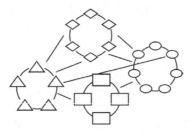

How things work: the modern organization is characterized by shared values and culture, transparent goals and projects, and the free flow of information and feedback. People are rewarded for their skills and abilities, not their position

Source: Deloitte (2017)

FLATARCHIES

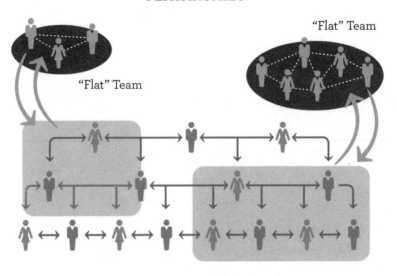

Source: Jacob Morgan (thefutureorganization.com, 2015)

Undoubtedly, we're not making the situation or challenge simpler, but we're getting to the truth of it: we need to design an organization with some degree of authoritative and domain-oriented structure, with immense focus on emerging small teams with a diverse set of internal structures, and with massive investment in the networks across the organization.

Let's look at how we do that.

We want to inspire
– and to start a movement.

We want to create a dialogue
around the modern workplace
based on empowerment,
innovation and trust.

————

Pia Verdich,
Head of LACE
(Lean–Agile Center of Excellence),
Ørsted

**Distributed leadership and
distributed decision-making**

CHAPTER 5.

HOW TO ORGANIZE THE WORKPLACE OF THE FUTURE

The key philosophy in this approach is to see the organization not as a pyramid with local functional areas that are streamlined for separate specialist areas, but as a **platform upon which local pockets of collaboration emerge, a modern Orange Platform for Teal Dots.**

A traditional, natural and often-seen development in organizational structure is the evolution from top-down pyramid to matrix to multiple separated pyramids and to inverted pyramids in a servant leadership style. What follows next in that development is **the platform of networked teams.**

> The role of the organizational fabric – the modern Orange World – is not to optimize for productivity and hierarchical distribution of responsibility and reporting, but to provide the right amount of support and nutrition to allow for spontaneous or guided emergence of self-governed and self-managed teams – the Teal Dots.
>
> On top of that platform, we nurture a network of cultural ambassadors, social anchors, communities of practice and knowledge hubs.
>
> The **role of the leaders** is to create this Orange World for the Teal Dots, to identify and nurture the mechanisms, and to lead this ecosystem.

Absolutely vital to this are two things: the modern leadership and the modern culture, both of which are undergoing paradigm shifts in mindset, skillset, behaviour and professionalism. You need an approach to designing and nurturing the Orange World, as the changes internally in the organization arise and when the megatrends in your business context hit you.

On the conceptual and mental level, this requires a shift in mindset, culture and identity – a change in definition and measurement of organizational cohesion and what success is. Massive work needs to be done here, hand in hand with practical changes to processes and mechanisms. Nothing happens in the training room alone. Nothing happens through PowerPoint and town hall meetings alone. This is daily hard work.

And, to begin with, you need these nine components in place:

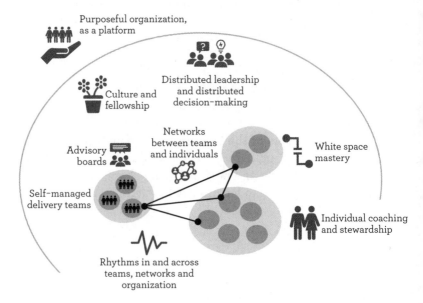

1. Purposeful organization, as a platform
2. Culture and fellowship
3. Individual coaching and stewardship
4. Distributed leadership and decision-making
5. Self-managed delivery teams
6. Advisory boards
7. Rhythms in and across teams, network and organization
8. White space mastery
9. Networks between teams and individuals

The following sections dive into each of these areas to describe the mindset, approach and design thinking required.

Part Four will explore practices, mechanisms and examples of each of these nine elements.

PURPOSEFUL ORGANIZATION, AS A PLATFORM

Purposeful organization, as a platform

How might we question:

How might we design and create a platform with a purposeful mission and an understandable strategy, where we make it possible for teams to genuinely collaborate (including with each other), where decisions are made at the right place and where people feel like showing up for work?

This is a fundamentally different approach to understanding what an organization is and what role it plays. The organization is seen as a platform for teams, as opposed to having a hierarchical structure or a pyramid-inside-a-pyramid reporting regime.

Two equally suitable approaches are trending:

Some leaders treat the teams and Teal Dots as start-ups or scaleups in their organization, approaching them as small businesses inside the business, with their own mission and business plan, their own board of directors (or advisory boards, as I prefer to describe them), their own P&L (profit and loss) responsibility, and their own strategy. The leaders make sure to understand and debate the maturity of the 'small businesses' in order to coach and mentor it accordingly, support it with finances and investment, provide access to suitable competencies and people, give it a mechanism for the distribution of tasks and projects (both within and between teams), and provide access to supportive group functions. In a sense, management act like venture capitalists and invest their time and money in the teams that have a great idea, drive and business justification. This also means that teams that do not have a good idea or business justification, or teams that have solved the problem they were originally created for, will be closed in a professional and non-problematic way.

Implementing this system can require massive change. Haier Group called it 'disruptive', as it changed its 70,000-employee organization over more than three decades. Disrupting the roles of employees, the organization and compensation, Haier split the company into 4,000 teams, or micro-enterprises (Corporate Rebels, 2019). However, this can be done on a smaller scale as well.

Other leaders place more of a focus on the fluidity of the organization, calling it 'organic culture' or 'an organism'. They are less focused on the hard splits into entities and interested in the humanistic approach to supporting teams and employees in self-management and self-governance. Trustworks and Pingala are examples of this approach, focusing on the culture and wellbeing of employees and less on the internal funding structures.

Both approaches have some clear similarities: they train the team in self-management and self-governance, and they have central institutions for handling that kind of training and coaching.

The beacon for the organization and thus for each and every team is the **purpose and meaningfulness** of the organization.

Understanding why you are here, what problem you solve for whom, what impact you are seeking to manifest and what value (functional, emotional or societal) you strive to create is the guidepost for all thinking, behaviour, prioritization, activities and reflections.

Focusing on the problems you are solving and not merely on the products is a central aspect of leadership and dialogue in the organizational modern Orange World. Set the direction, describe and vocalize the strategy, share your dream and let the teams handle the details.

Describe this purpose and meaning to employees and customers in the same room and make space and time for them to shape and grow the team and find the solution (and the product) together.

On the practical side, becoming a Teal Dot in an Orange World involves a shift in how classic corporate group functions are designed: people and culture, legal, finance, IT, service management, project management offices, purchasing, etc. All of these corporate functions change their role and self-perception from mandatory-to-use corporate functions to service-oriented business partners to the teams, the leaders and the employees. They establish service catalogues and run internal marketing activities to offer themselves and their contributions to the teams. End-to-end business understanding is vital for these service areas, and increasing amounts of focus and effort are being invested in relationship-building between the business units and the shared services. Currently in Denmark, the HR and IT areas are the frontrunners in this, with a massive focus on the business partner/bridgebuilder role and on being present in the line of business.

One other vital element here is the continued obligation to **ensure that employees have a 'home' where they belong – either HR related or professionally.** This is where the employees have their long-term base, where their macro-oriented development occurs, and where their legal and HR commitment is situated. It is also where they negotiate their salary and have their regular wellbeing conversations.

The platform structure also nurtures communities of practice for professional development and sparring. In modern organizations, professional sparring happens in two variants: in domain-ordered hierarchical groups or in communities of interest, excellence or practice. In both cases the sparring is initiated and driven by the Orange Platform.

And, finally, distributed authority in hierarchical levels is still in place, in selected high-impact areas: To support the Teal Dots, **a scaffolding of structure is present**, that ultimately has responsivity for things that are universal to the life of organization. These decisions and responsibilities have a more sluggish or sticker rate of movement, and higher inertia and higher risk; and require a very board insight to the market and the stakeholder landscape. This rough distribution of responsibility and authority makes sure that the mission and purpose of the organization are right and clear, that communication and dialogue across the organization takes place, that the cross-organizational core business processes or value streams are in place, that quality and compliance aspects are handled correctly and uniformly, that decisions are made at the right location, etc. In general, the scaffolding or hierarchy ensures that the framework for the Orange organization and for the Teal Dots is in place:

- **Why** are we here? What is our purpose?
- **Who** are we? What are our culture and virtues?
- **What** meaningful goals are we pursuing?
- **How** do we plan to get there? What is our strategy?

Please note, that formulating the strategy and the subsequent tactical intention for executing the strategy is handled via the rhythm of business. See later in this chapter.

The organization-as-a-platform mindset is a crucial design approach to how modern organizations identify themselves and to how the leadership develops.

CULTURE AND FELLOWSHIP

Culture and fellowship

How might we question:

How might we discover and nurture the culture that is fitting for a team-of-teams thinking, with cross-organizational/cross-team networks and with fruitful synergy between the individual and the collective tribe?

The organizational culture in the future of work is one of connectedness, communities and belonging. In an emergent organizational design with multiple local Teal Dots in an Orange World, understanding what culture is, how to describe and debate it, and how to align expectations to behaviour and give feedback on misaligned or even wrong behaviour is an increasingly local and diverse activity. This means that two seemingly opposite forces are at play.

On the one hand, you need an organizational culture that creates **identity** and **fellowship** for all employees. This identity and fellowship can be used for collaboration between teams and at the interfaces of business processes, and they can serve as the norm for how you interact with partners and subcontractors and how you deliver products and services to customers.

On the other hand, you need leeway and mental acceptance for local **differences** between the teams in terms of how they practice the culture, how they work and talk, how they make agreements, etc.

You need a culture that ensures alignment across the organization and is built for autonomy in teams. A place where people want to show up. A place where there is psychological safety.

BUILDING A MODERN CULTURE OF ALIGNMENT
AND AUTONOMY

Organizational culture emerges from four things alone: what we do, what we say, what we experience and how those three things make us feel. Martin Seligman, the godfather of positive psychology, formulated the PERMA model (Seligman, 2011) for what people need to experience in order to grow: positive emotion, engagement, relationships, meaning and accomplishments.

To support this PERMA culture, you need to build relationships, transparency, diversity, empowerment and trust. The organizational culture in the Orange World is one of belonging and fellowship, in order to create the required mix of alignment and autonomy. The Orange World is a key to driving and nurturing this experience.

There has been a clear shift in cultural expectations over the past 50 years, as simplified and summarized by Gallup (2016) in this overview.

Past	Future
My paycheck	My purpose
My satisfaction	My development
My boss	My coach
My annual review	My ongoing conversations
My weaknesses	My strengths
My job	My life

Over the past decade, the millennial mindset has spread across age groups and generation gaps. It no longer only pertains to millennials! More employees want to experience the millennial kind of workplace (Krautwald, 2018).

Corporate Rebels (2017) has listed eight habits of great organizations. Such organizations change and develop their mindset and mechanisms:
1. From profit to purpose and values
2. From hierarchical pyramids to a network of teams
3. From directive leadership to supportive leadership
4. From predict and plan to experiment and adapt
5. From rules and control to freedom and trust
6. From centralized authority to distributed authority
7. From secrecy to radical transparency
8. From job descriptions to talents and mastery

What we really want is a combination of the old and new; of the past approach and the future requirements. It is not either-or, but a mix. They augment each other, and your leadership task is to understand the nuances and apply them when needed.

Not only is this a guideline for modern leadership but it also describes the cultural behaviours and expectations of modern employees (Morgan, 2017). The connection to culture and fellowship is obvious: you need to build a culture of relationships, transparency, diversity, empowerment and trust. **Fellowship** based on connectedness, mutual interests, and genuine candour is at the core of the identity of this kind of organization: people like to show up, and they engage in the culture.

As documented in a study among more than 19,000 workers across the globe by ADP Research Institute (2019), being in a team and having trust in the team lead are vital to engagement at work.

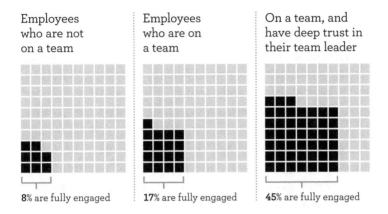

Employees who are not on a team	Employees who are on a team	On a team, and have deep trust in their team leader
8% are fully engaged	**17%** are fully engaged	**45%** are fully engaged

"The share of employees who are fully engaged more than doubles if they are on a team. It more than doubles again if they strongly trust the team leader"
(Buckingham and Goodall, 2019).

Source: Buckingham and Goodall (2019) based on data
from ADP Research Institute (2019).

The key to developing your culture is not power but influence, which starts with an authentic approach to the people you surround yourself with. Via networking, building relationships, giving and asking for feedback, and engaging with your employees, you begin building the foundation of a culture that is resilient, responsive and inclusive.

CULTURE IN A MULTI-DIVERSE SETTING

When a team grows to more than 10-15 employees, subcultures and fractions emerge naturally, since interaction fatigue kicks in (Küblböck, 2019). It is hard to maintain dialogue and friendly connections with many colleagues, and local team dynamics emerge. According to psychological scientists such as Robin Dunbar (1998), the same thing happens when a tribe reaches 80-150 people. Subcultures emerge, more formalized processes are needed and the Orange Platform is needed. This is all natural.

This means two things, though. First, the organization must encourage the teams to debate, describe and develop their local culture, and, second, the organization must embrace and acknowledge local differences in culture. If you encourage the teams to be self-managed, you also encourage them to shape their own culture. The differences may be minuscule and negligible in relation to the organizational culture, but they could be major or even so radical that you need to consider intervening and realigning a team with the rest. The key point here is that you as a leader must handle both dimensions of the cultural work – the cross-organizational Orange culture and the local Teal culture – and be responsive and supportive of their work.

This is exactly where fellowship and mutual obligations are created and negotiated on a daily basis.

Several of the new SALT (see Chapter 2) organizational structures have built-in mechanisms for reflection and best practices for inclusive dialogue. For example, sociocracy and holacracy use so-called consent or rounds for equivalence and equality in the humanistic approach to inclusion, and Scrum uses the retrospective for reflection on the collaboration. Both mechanisms nurture frequent and regular efforts towards self-understanding in the team culture and support the team in developing and maintaining its self-management.

ADDING TO COMPLEXITY AND DIVERSITY

To all of the above must be added the complexity of working with colleagues with different personal profiles, in different time zones, in different locations, from different national cultures. This complexity underlines the importance of constantly understanding and proactively describing the virtues and best-practice behaviours that the team instils and agrees upon.

The Teal Dots in the Orange World will inevitably have differences. You must encourage these differences to help each team discover its own interpretation so as to enable autonomy as team members but alignment and fellowship in the team. At the same time, you must enable autonomy in the team and alignment and fellowship as an organization.

This is your cultural task. For the Teal Dot: create autonomy as a team member and alignment inside the team. For the Orange World: create autonomy as a team and alignment inside the organization.

These concepts recall the alignment/autonomy matrix introduced in Chapter 2.

INDIVIDUAL COACHING AND STEWARDSHIP

Individual coaching and stewardship

How might we question:

How might we handle personal wellbeing and professional development in a Teal Dot where the daily interactions are many, and in an Orange World with far fewer interactions? Who has the responsibility, and how do we handle it?

Because of this pivotal redesign of the organization and how the teams interact with each other, several people processes must be redesigned. It is especially necessary to redesign the ways in which care and charity are shown to individual employees, in order to fit with the multitude of touchpoints and team dynamics that each employee is a part of.

The organization needs updated approaches to its daily sparring, support and feedback; to the regular personal development conversation; to career paths; to hiring and firing; to onboarding; to promotions and shifts in roles; and to incentive structures and salary models. The overall design criterion is a balance between (a) local belonging in a team, (b) professional anchoring in a community of practice and (c) company-wide identity.

Coaching and mentoring will need to be split into two dimensions: between the line manager in the Orange World and the delivery manager in the Teal Dot.

- On the Orange Platform, the employee has a 'home ground' in the communities of practice that the manager builds and nurtures. This is where the employees' professional and long-term development happens, and where they feel at home. This can be called **macro coaching**.
- The employee enters one or more Teal delivery teams, where the Teal delivery manager has responsibility for the employees' daily wellbeing and skill mastery. This can be called **micro coaching**.

This means that each employee and leader must experience daily touchpoints with the team members and with the cultural leads in the team, and fewer regular check-ins and touchpoints with the representatives of the communities of practice, whether those are leaders, subject matter experts or relevant members dispersed in the local Teal Dots. This requires careful design and experimentation and is under constant reconstruction to honour the individual compositions of the Teal Dots, the teams of teams and the network.

Several organizations are experimenting with radical changes to the traditional HR schemes, abolishing the annual appraisal conversation and bell-curve evaluation mechanisms.

Instead, they are creating **formal stewardship** by increasing the frequency of the check-in touchpoints to weekly or bi-weekly, and by holding quarterly in-depth conversations where the line manager makes sure to gather input from all relevant stakeholders and colleagues that provides perspective on the employees' behaviour and performance. This means that the line manager might need to talk to as many as five or more colleagues whom the employee has indicated as connection points or collaboration partners. Several organizations use software platforms to make this perspective gathering smooth and efficient.

Others go even further, enabling employees to select their own mentor and their own manager from whom they want coaching on personal or professional aspects of their work. Or, they conduct an organizational network analysis on an annual basis to map the relationships between employees on different professional and social aspects and use the results to couple pairs of mentors and mentees. In this way, they create **self-propelled stewardship**.

Clearly this means that every leader – and often every employee too – needs to be trained in coaching and mentoring, and there should be an organization-wide approach to supporting this mechanism with templates and guidelines.

A final note on employee development in Teal Dots within an Orange World is that the competency set for employees undergoes expansion. First of all, developments in technology and society means that new business skills are needed from employees. McKinsey Global Institute documented that the demand for higher cognitive skills, social and emotional skills, and technological skills (see the examples in the table over the page) is dramatically rising (Bughin et al., 2018).

Higher cognitive skills	Social and emotional skills	Technological skills
• Advanced literacy and writing • Quantitative and statistical skills • Critical thinking and decision-making • Project management • Complex information-processing and interpretation • Creativity	• Advanced communication and negotiation skills • Interpersonal skills and empathy • Leadership and managing others • Entrepreneurship and initiative-taking • Adaptability and continuous learning • Teaching and training others	• Basic digital skills • Advanced IT skills and programming • Advanced data analysis and mathematical skills • Technology design, engineering and maintenance • Scientific research and development

Second, the competencies of an employee in this kind of organism are different from those required of an employee in the classic hierarchical structure. There will be added focus on aspects such as end-to-end business understanding; lateral thinking and problem-solving; organic relationship-building, active listening and nonverbal communication; mastering change management; emotional intelligence; and personal insight. These are skills that are needed to navigate in a complex, dynamic world with many different colleagues and contexts.

This puts extra focus on the coaching and mentoring skillset of the leader and those who are appointed as stewards. It is *essential* for these people to master emotional intelligence and empathy and the ability to create psychological safety. Leadership, culture and coaching are relentlessly interwoven.

DISTRIBUTED LEADERSHIP AND
DISTRIBUTED DECISION-MAKING

Distributed leadership and distributed decision-making

How might we question:

How might we make sure that decisions are taken at the right time, by the right people, with the right information? How do we handle decision-making in a VUCA world? How do we create a culture where the Teal Dots willingly commit to making decisions, where the old decision makers refrain from making decisions, and where mistakes are accepted?

The role of the leadership, especially of top management, must shift from being in the hands of a single person to being a team activity.

The team of teams and networked dynamics together form the answer to the challenge of navigating, gathering enough data and making prioritizations in a VUCA world (see Chapter 1) with an increasing pace of development, technological shifts and constant changes. In a volatile, uncertain, complex and ambiguous business world, embodying leadership and handling change are like yin and yang. You need to be more alert so as to listen and respond to the frequent and massive changes. But the old top-management approach of making an informed decision based on personal experience within the domain and on personal market understanding is inadequate. Increasingly, you do not have time to figure the issue out yourself or will not be able to afford to from a business perspective.

You need to base your decision-making on less data and instead rely on newfound creativity in the organization.

The only way to do that is to distribute leadership and decision-making to your peers and employees, and to create a diversity of thinkers and decision makers. A more diverse team will have better debates, find new questions and answers, and see new opportunities – and make better decisions, faster.

What directly follows from that is a stronger and more coherent change management approach. Obviously, this is partially because the ones who are part of making the change happen and executing the ideas are involved in the decision-making. But it is also because the awareness and dialogue activities in any change management approach (either linear or emergent) are built into the decision-making to a certain extent, especially if the organization's influencers and subject matter experts are involved in the debate, problem clarification and decisions. The more we place the decision mandate with those who have the appropriate merits and are the professional and social gravity points in the organization, the better decisions we get and the better anchored they are.

Leadership will be something that more people are encouraged to take part in, focusing on the following two things:

First, **setting direction**, ensuring that the organization gathers energy and forces to solve the same problem, together. The organization must focus on doing the right things and on ensuring that the organization knows what 'right' is – that is, the virtues and ethics of the organizational behaviour. Also, the leadership must make sure that the organization creates value and follows up on it.

In turn, this means that leaders in the modern Orange World must ensure that the teams (the Teal Dots) get sufficient space and time to do things right. The skill to master this task as a team strongly depends on the maturity of the team.

It is the leader's role to coach and mentor the team according to the maturity of the team and with situational leadership on the team level in mind.

Second, **distributing decision-making** means understanding the difference between authority (formal or meritocracy based) and authorization (what we are allowed to decide). It is key here to empower teams with the responsibility, courage and habits needed to make decisions locally, partly because it is the right thing to do but also to instil in them the wherewithal to know when they should be seeking relevant advice first.

A survey conducted by the Danish organization Center for Ledelse (Centre for Leadership) shows that organizations with distributed decision-making experience increased their financial profit over a three-year period, whereas the exact opposite was the case when decision-making was centralized to the manager for the area (Center for Ledelse, 2019).

The crucial point here is to encourage a continuous dialogue between the distribution parties, whether they are peers in the leadership team or advisory boards to the team. This is because only some decisions can be described and designed as rule-based decisions or rule-based delegation. Admittedly, some can, and a tool such as the delegation board is a phenomenal visual aid for periodic review of the overall grand scheme for how decisions are distributed.

However, more frequently, I find that exception-based decision-making is clogging the traditional organizational bandwidth. This means that timely availability of leaders in the modern Orange World is vital to the teams for them to have access to sparring and input on matters that are outside their comfort zone. Modern Teams must be trained in acknowledging where their comfort zone is, and they must be comfortable with approaching the advisory board or other subject matter experts with their questions or a decision to be made.

In order to make this happen, the organization and its culture need to have a basis of psychological safety. Leaders must shape the identity and culture of the organization, both internally and externally, to ensure that decisions are made in the right places by those who have the necessary insight and outlook. This approach means change in four areas:

1. Top leaders must stop making decisions and allow teams to make them. This is a change in identity from being at the centre of the world and the oracle of all knowledge to being a facilitator. Some people really struggle with this.

2. Teams must accept, embrace and feel comfortable with making decisions that have actual impact. To some, that power is something they cannot and will not handle. The concrete level of decision-making and mandate is thus a matter of distribution between the team and its advisory board or leaders.

3. Mistakes will happen, and that is okay. When you shift the decision-making power to the Teal Dots, decisions will be made that you might disagree with, and faulty decisions will be made. You must come to terms with both scenarios and create the needed psychological safety.

4. Customers need to understand and learn (a) that it is not always the top manager or the key account manager who makes the decisions, and the team and its members are fully qualified and empowered to do so, and (b) that escalating issues might not have any effect, as the top management does not have the necessary insight to get involved and wants to enforce the philosophy of distributed decision-making.

Widen's 'no escalation' principle

Widen has been a WorldBlu certified organization
for five years (2015-2019). WorldBlu's 'Freedom
at Work' approach (see WorldBlu.com) describes a
philosophy for organizational democracy based on
ten principles that lead to freedom, engagement,
safety and trust in the workplace:

1. Purpose + Vision
2. Transparency
3. Dialogue + Listening
4. Fairness + Dignity
5. Accountability
6. Individual + Collective
7. Choice
8. Integrity
9. Decentralization
10. Reflection + Evaluation.

It is clear that distributed leadership and distributed
decision-making are integrated effects of working
in an organizational democracy, according to the
ten principles above.

Matthew Gonnering, CEO of Widen and winner
of the 2019 Executive of the Year award from
In Business magazine, stands firm on the
organization's 'no escalation' principle. Gonnering
has an email template ready for cases where a
customer escalates an issue above the team level.
The template states that escalation will not help
solve the issue, will not give the right answer, will
be a waste of time and will not be fast enough.
Gonnering himself describes the approach:

The standard approach stemmed from an interaction we had with a customer who escalated their way through the organization when the person who had the knowledge to answer the question was already on the front line and very capable of making proper prioritization decisions. The customer assumed we were structured with rigid hierarchy like them and executive involvement would reprioritize work and create greater urgency.

We did not have a good way to prevent this type of escalation within our process, so we authored text to help guide future customer executive requests. The statement we provided our front-line teams is as follows and can be modified as they see fit:

"Our internal structure is an organizational democracy, which means escalation is just bringing unnecessary people into the thread. We are empowered to act in your best interest without executive attention or approval. I look forward to sharing this story with our executive team once we get it resolved. Now, back to the issue at hand."

Gonnering trusts the teams, and he releases the issue back to the place where it rightfully can and must be solved – between the team and the customer.

Part Three of this book elaborates on leadership, and Part Four dives into practices and mechanisms.

SELF-MANAGED DELIVERY TEAMS

Self-managed delivery teams

How might we question:

How might we design the modern Orange World such that the Teal Dots can emerge and dissolve when needed, and such that they can be adequately self-managed, considering their maturity as a team?

Your organization must have an approach for the **life cycle** of the Teal Dots. When do they emerge – and why? Who creates them? What defines a team? What framework do they work and live in? When are they done and when can they dissolve themselves? And what exactly is meant by 'self-managed teams'?

Please note that this book does not go into detail about internal team dynamics. That area is covered by a vast literature already. This book focuses on what happens between and around teams.

According to Frédéric Laloux, Teal organizations "are seen as living entities, oriented towards realizing their potential. ... Self-management replaces hierarchical pyramid" (Laloux, 2015). Key words for organizations' self-understanding are 'living organism', 'self-management', 'wholeness' and 'evolutionary purpose'. And these words can be used for teams themselves too, not only for the full organization.

Self-managed delivery teams

Self-managed: The ability to and engagement in doing the right things and doing the things right, and with the empowerment, authority and authorization to make the right decisions at the right time – depending on the maturity of the team and with suitable situation-based support from the advisory board.

Delivery: Contextual end-to-end responsibility for delivery of the service or product.

Team: A group of people working together and depending on each other with a shared purpose, shared goal, shared plan, shared understanding of individual roles, and shared approach to continuous reflection and improvement.

Teams that fully live up to the definition above "are seen as living entities, oriented towards realizing their potential," and they need constant but situational support, depending on their current shape and mental energy (Laloux, 2015).

Note that the notion 'self-managed' will create controversy if not handled correctly. As Christian Ørsted writes in his bestseller *Lethal Leadership* (2013), self-management can lead to anxiety and stress, without proper expectation management regarding deliverables and behaviour.
Do not engage your teams in self-management without the required framework for psychological safety, dialogue and expectation management.
Never leave the team alone.

The responsibility of modern leadership is to create a framework and supporting mechanisms for the dynamics of such teams, their maturity and their life cycle. You should create an Orange World that the teams can live in – teams that are of different shapes, that are at different levels of maturity and that have different needs for support.

This also means that a fitting and context-dependent amount of self-management or self-governance should be an integral part of the team's identity: all teams need the right amount of leeway, empowerment, self-management and room for decision-making.

The key phrase here is 'the right amount', which is vital for the dynamics of the whole organization. This approach is responsive to internal and external changes, and the interconnected ecosystem of employees and stakeholders must understand this and adjust accordingly.

Several aspects are needed for this to happen:
- A framework for the establishment and reflection of teams
- An understanding and acceptance of the diversity of internal team structures
- A differentiated approach to the maturity of self-management
- An approach to distributing tasks and information to the teams
- Regular support from the surrounding organization, employees and leaders, e.g. in the form of advisory boards

Teams must have end-to-end accountability for their task, and the ability to define and agree on scope and expected quality (with the guidance of the advisory board). For Teal teams, the formal design of an organization is not important. Solving the problem is.

Few organizations are used to teams being formed of the members' own volition and most do not find it an intuitive process, so the majority of organizations need training and a shared approach, as understandings and expectations regarding how teamwork and interpersonal collaboration should be handled are highly individual. Therefore, it is important to have a common approach to forming, evaluating and dissolving teams.

THE DIVERSITY OF TEAMS AND TEAL DOTS

When aiming to establish this approach, it is very important to acknowledge the diversity of the internal structures of the Teal Dots. Not all tasks are suitable for a flat, organized team. And not all people are comfortable with being in a fully self-managed team.

Operations and maintenance, for example, need predictability and repetition, so they suit a structure with a clear hierarchy and chains of command, with standard operating procedures, and with stringency. Similarly, explorative and fast-changing project work fits well with a flat, dynamic, experimenting network structure. And, of course, the same principles apply for individual employees. **Some like structure and thrive in it. Some like the bohemian nonconformity of a loosely coupled team.** Jacob Morgan has termed this approach the 'flatarchy' (Morgan, 2015), a term that describes organizations that are not purely hierarchical and not purely flat, but a suitable mix of the two worlds.

A way to approach this mix is to use the manifesto of Responsive Org (see Responsive.org) as a platform for dialogue both within the teams and between the team and the ecosystem that it interacts with (stakeholders, sponsors, managers, subject matter experts, other teams, etc.): sliders can be introduced between the opposites in the manifesto, and the resulting tool can be used for expectation management and clarification of individual preferences.

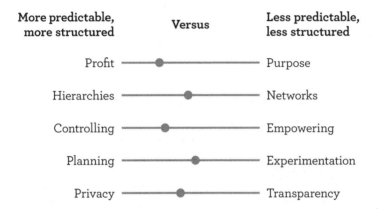

More predictable, more structured	Versus	Less predictable, less structured
Profit	—●—	Purpose
Hierarchies	—●—	Networks
Controlling	—●—	Empowering
Planning	—●—	Experimentation
Privacy	—●—	Transparency

The manifesto of Responsive Org can be used as a tool for expectation management for a team, by adding sliders to connect the opposites in the manifesto. Consider: how should your team balance each of the opposite pairs? What are your preferences – and what are the expectations of the stakeholders and collaborative parties in the team's ecosystem? Use the tool internally in the team, inside the organization with the advisory board (see also next section), and externally, for example with your sponsor, your steering committee or your customers.

Regardless of the specific outcome of this exercise, after you carry it out, the modern organization and the Orange World will be capable of supporting you far better, as the team and the ecosystem will have obtained knowledge about the potential diversity of opinions and the different needs for interaction and information. In that sense, the team will become aware of the degree of self-management required and the need for support from the surrounding culture.

Whatever the internal structure of the team (hierarchical or networked), the **culture and identity** of such a self-managed team are nurtured through a coaching approach to the life cycle and maturity of the team, as described via situational leadership from the advisory board or the leaders.

ADVISORY BOARDS TO THE TEAL DOTS

Advisory boards

How might we question:

How might we support teams in the best possible way, such that they have the right amount of self-management and still feel connected to the surrounding leadership and culture? How do we design advisory boards that can provide day-to-day input to the team?

Every team needs support. The nature of this support changes over time, depending on the team's maturity, internal conflicts, unforeseen challenges, mistakes and defects, changes in assignments, prioritizations, etc. The support can be regular and daily, or on-demand and infrequent, but every team needs support from the culture, the organization, the leadership authorities and colleagues. Never leave the team alone.

Based on an assessment of the teams and the organizational culture, advisory boards can be appointed. The use of advisory boards is a fundamentally different approach to leadership than the traditional reporting-oriented management and steering committees that exist in corporate organizations.

The role of advisory boards is to provide the minimum but right amount of advice, input, coaching, support and instruction to the teams, based on their maturity and the situation they are in. Boards should show direction and then get out of the way. They must support, coach and guide the teams; remove impediments; and handle access to resources, experts, competencies and stakeholders. Their focus should be on impact and outcome measurements, not on output. This also means that the members of advisory boards must be people with genuine knowledge and experience. They can be solution architects, subject matter experts, salespersons or some other relevant role. They do not have to be leaders.

The advisory board is not a reporting board. The purpose of the advisory board is to enable the team to commit to the end-to-end delivery or service and to take care of each other. The advisory board is not responsible for the delivery (the team is responsible for that) but for the team itself (the individual team members, the team culture, and the team's wellbeing and healthy dynamics) and for ensuring that the team is 'doing the right thing' in accordance with the organizational purpose and culture and the company strategy.

This is highly contextual and dynamic and should be assessed and adjusted regularly.

AN APPROACH TO MATURITY AND ALIGNMENT
ON THE ORGANIZATIONAL AND TEAM LEVELS

Inherent in the awareness of how you design, form and run your organization is the embrace of differences in the structures and maturity of teams: your Teal Dots will have different internal design and collaboration mechanisms, based on the mindsets of the individual team members and on the mindset of the team.

Across the organization, you need a way to sense and debate the maturity of the organization and the individual teams, and how they relate to the spectrum of Orange and Teal. You need to establish and actively use a modern maturity assessment mechanism to provide the individual teams with the opportunity to reflect on their identity, approach to collaboration and engagement, and level of self-management. Consider using the Maturity Assessment (presented in Chapter 3).

You need a clear way to describe and debate purpose, identity, reasoning, innovation, approach to development, culture, self-organization and self-management, and leadership, so that you can coach and support the teams in the way that they need.

In so doing, you can create a heat map of your organization and apply the proper amounts of coaching and support to both the organizational culture and the individual teams.

SELF-MANAGEMENT AND SITUATIONAL LEADERSHIP FOR TEAMS

Depending on the maturity of the team (or Teal Dot), the need for your presence as a leader and as a member of the advisory board will evolve over time. Just as situational leadership (Hersey and Blanchard, 1969) is applied and used for coaching, supporting, instructing and motivating individual employees, situational leadership applies to teams too.

If a team is immature and newly formed and cannot manage itself, you need to supply attention. On the other hand, the more self-managed and mature a team is, the less attention you need to supply.

High

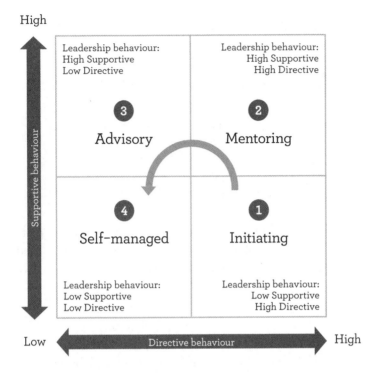

Low

Situational leadership for teams.

Source: Adapted from Hersey and Blanchard (1969) to focus on supporting
the development and maturity of Teal Dots in an Orange World.

The best-functioning advisory boards consist of two,
or a maximum of three, experienced employees from the
organization who have business understanding, interpersonal and humanistic skills, and enough technical and
project management insight to provide advice and sparring.
The best advisory boards are good at asking questions and
careful when it comes to giving teams answers too quickly.

WHITE SPACE MASTERY

White space mastery

How might we question:

How might we spot the challenges or opportunities that no one has seen yet? How do we ensure that relevant experiences and lessons are shared across teams and units?

Once you have initiated new ways of working and Teal Dots start to emerge, a new challenge and unprecedented need arises: the need for white space mastery.

> White space mastery is inspired by white space management, a concept described by Rummler and Brache (1990) as the area between the boxes in an organizational chart, where very often no one is in charge.
>
> It is also where "rules are vague, authority is fuzzy, budgets are non-existent, and strategy is unclear" (Minzberg et al., 1988, p. 419).

The theory and design thinking that lead to the existence of an organizational Orange Platform that teams can live on carry with them a built-in challenge: **understanding and mastering the unknown and undiscovered things that happen – or don't happen – between the teams.**

The more self-managed and self-propelled the Teal Dots are, the less they are part of a governance structure.

This entails a risk of having autonomous but unaligned teams. They could end up working solo without a cross-organizational rhythm, or being outside the functional ecosystem (which then cannot support them) and the shared company culture.

Examples of issues that can arise from such a situation are decisions that have no owner, product requests that no one has discovered or exploited, scope that no one has thought of, initiatives that are not harvested, 'under the radar'-work that is not used, and rumours, politics and team goals that are counter-productive.

The way to mitigate this risk of ending up with unaligned or misaligned teams is threefold:

1. Establish white space mastery
2. Establish rhythms of business and connections
3. Establish networks and ecosystems between teams and between individuals

These measures will ensure alignment between teams while still maintaining and nurturing their autonomy.

Naturally, there are two extremely important premises that need to be in place for this to succeed. First, there must be widespread understanding among the teams of your organization's purpose and reason for existing and, second, your organization's culture must focus on fellowship. Without these premises, alignment is nearly impossible to obtain and nurture.

Leaders who intuitively have the ability to master white space are those who see the blind spots of the organization and strive to close the gap by investigating, analysing, suggesting an approach and facilitating a decision. Key to the ability to do this is a holistic mindset and an understanding of the internal organization and the dynamics of execution. It is also important to be able to predict the behaviour of internal stakeholders and know their strengths, as this helps the white space manager to find and uncover issues and possibilities.

> Several of the modern leaders I have met who are true masters of white space have similar psychological profiles, with strong professional drive and ambition and immense emotional intelligence (EQ).
>
> They have a sense for spotting issues that have not manifested themselves yet, for identifying uncovered development, for intuitively bringing information forward to other relevant contexts, for zooming out and looking at the big picture, and for pattern-matching both laterally and horizontally, across time and teams.

White space mastery is not a game of spotting mistakes or playing devil's advocate. On the contrary, it is about exploiting as-yet-unexploited territory, or avoiding conflict that otherwise would have been unavoidable.

The organizations that create a truly modern Orange World for Teal teams and for engaged individuals appreciate and encourage behaviour that ensures alignment. White space mastery is one of the critical elements in doing that. Most often, white space mastery is handled by strong, networked individuals, but increasingly this skill is seen as a cultural trait rather than an individual task.

A way to approach and accommodate the goals of white space mastery is to seek dialogue and information-sharing frequently. You should strive to understand patterns of behaviour and thought, and the strengths of the managers and key influencers in your organization. The goal is to jointly create a full picture of the situation and to find the things that fall between the cracks, together.

There are two possible approaches to this: first, have individual employees who act as **information liaisons** between teams or, second, have a culture of 'working out loud', where all employees take part in sharing their work, their challenges and their problem-solving approaches. Social media platforms are excellent for this kind of white space mastery and knowledge-sharing, as long as it is carried out on a professional basis.

However, white space mastery must be augmented and supported by a focus on wellbeing, psychological safety and interpersonal skills, since issues, latent conflicts, and opportunities for development and cross-pollination of soft skills rarely surface through working-out-loud mechanisms without facilitation and trust.

Organizations and leaders that master white space are clearly in a class above the rest. It is a game changer for the engagement and wellbeing of employees.

RHYTHMS IN AND ACROSS TEAMS, NETWORKS AND ORGANIZATION

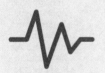

Rhythms in and across teams, networks and organization

How might we question:

How might we design a rhythm of business and rhythm of connections such that tactical execution happens in the right places, activities are in sync, information flows between the right sources, people are engaged and developing, employee challenges and opportunities are addressed, and changes and adaptations are handled across the organization?

One of the benefits of releasing teams from the hierarchical structure is their opportunity for self-management. Clearly, in a business world that is challenged with regard to embracing new technology and updated societal and humane megatrends, a significantly higher degree of adaptability and local freedom is needed. This creates autonomy but also gives birth to a new challenge, namely alignment.

Alignment and synchronization across teams, departments and business units are obviously harder to achieve when you do not have the classic command-and-control, top-down approach to sharing information; deciding on tactical activities, funding and sponsorship; distributing tasks and resources; assigning tasks to teams; and following up on status and progress. With the absence of these structures, we replace **cascade**-based dialogue with **cadence**-based dialogue.

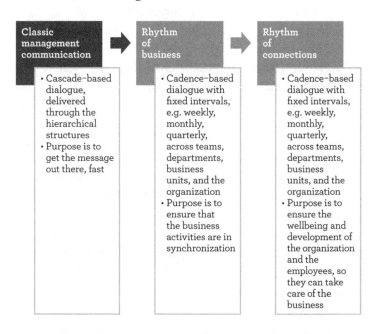

The modern organization changes its approach to synchronization and alignment to be cadence-based, not cascade-based. This rhythm is the responsibility of the Orange World that the Teal Dots live in.

Teal Dots observation number 3:

Tactical execution happens when touchpoints
are frequent and physical

The term 'rhythm' refers to having a synchronized way of working and meeting in and across teams. Typically, this is done via meetings with fixed intervals, for example weekly, monthly or quarterly, taking place across teams, departments, business units and the organization. The analogy is that of a band or orchestra, playing at the same tempo, in sync with each other but with room for improvisation.

It is important to keep the touchpoints physical, with face-to-face dialogue and visual artefacts (whiteboard, large posters, scrum board, etc.) to create the best possible collaboration and co-ordination.

RHYTHM OF BUSINESS

Rhythm is pivotal to the synchronization of the business activities in the organization, and to their ability to stay relevant to the market and to each other. This ensures that the purpose, the strategic dreams, the tactical execution and the operational manifestation of activities are aligned. The rhythm of business handles your value chain, key processes and quality governance, and ensures delivery of your services and products.

This approach is heavily inspired by the agile methodology (Agile Alliance, 2001), especially the Scrum-inspired mechanism where a fixed-length sprint of two to four weeks is the core of the planning-and-execution time horizon (Sutherland, 2014): the team members agree on what to do in the upcoming period of time, they split up to perform their tasks, and they reassemble by the end of the period to show and tell what they have produced and learned, and to agree their intention for the next period.

When this approach is scaled horizontally across the organization and business units to cover several teams, frameworks such as SAFe (Scaled Agile Framework) provide inspiration and guidance in designing the approach, offering concepts such as master planning, quarterly sprints across the business units and tactical execution. Local sprints (of, say, three weeks) will be contained in megasprints across the business (of, say, three months) to ensure synchronization.

The key take-aways point in the three directions of synchronization of business deliverables are as follows:

1. Top down: Ensure that we do the right things
2. Horizontally, across teams: Ensure that we do the right things right
3. Bottom up: Ensure that impact, output and outcome support the business' purpose, and ensure that learning about collaboration and production dependencies is shared

This then also means that the rhythm of business is the mechanism where the strategy is formulated, the tactical intention is designed and aligned, and where the follow-up sessions are facilitated. Like how alignment of activities in the SALT organizational designs are handled, the strategic and tactical mechanisms in the modern Orange World take place with involvement of the right people at the right level, and at the right time. It's aligned, but with local autonomy.

Vital to the success of this approach is how the leadership insists on the rhythm, and how the Orange World supports the culture, process, dialogue, synchronization, and reflection on collaboration and production.

RHYTHM OF CONNECTIONS

Whereas the rhythm of business is about production, the rhythm of connections is about people.

The more developed, mature and advanced your organization becomes, the more you will see autonomy and alignment starting to take care of the business synchronization. This does not happen spontaneously, of course, but is driven, nurtured and enabled by the Orange World – the culture, leadership and mechanisms that fill the gaps between the teams.

Richard Branson, founder of Virgin Group, is claimed to have said, "Clients do not come first. Employees come first. If you take care of your employees, they will take care of the clients." This is exactly what the rhythm of connections is about: taking care of people, culture, organizational development and changes, reorganizations, relationships, personal development, stakeholder relations, challenges, opportunities and changes.

Like the approach from rhythm of business, the design of the rhythm of connections is fixed and frequent. Daily and weekly team meetings, bi-weekly personal one-to-ones, monthly department meetings and bi-weekly leadership meetings (and management meetings across several teams or departments) are examples of such meetings. The closer together they are in the network and the more relevant the parties are to each other, the higher frequency is needed.

Rhythm, listening, adjustments and organic changes are the key mechanisms in sustaining a cross-organizational competence in collaboration. Closeness, relevance and frequency of touchpoints are correlated in this setup. Predictability and steady rhythm are at the centre here, in somewhat contradiction to the responsiveness that are obtained from them.

IN PRACTICE

One of the things that sets some businesses and leadership cultures apart from the rest is their ability to collaborate horizontally or across the networked organization. I see this all the time in the companies that I study and work with: those business units and teams that establish and maintain a high-frequency method of dialogue, task sharing, collaboration, learning and handshakes across teams and individuals clearly have an advantage over their peers.

The higher the frequency of the touchpoints, the more likely you are to exploit the synergy of your teams and to avoid prolonged correction of mistakes and misunderstandings. And, the better you master the rhythm of business, the more you can and should focus on and embrace the rhythm of connections.

Mikko Laukka, Executive Vice President of Risk Analytics at Danske Bank (a Danish bank with approximately 19,000 employees) and the bank's leadership team show a strong example of how to do this. Since 2015, they have worked deliberately to create new ways of working, a flatter hierarchy, a culture of people first and a purposeful platform for the bank's teams to live on. Their management meetings have developed over time, following the spirit of the massive cultural journey they have been on and in alignment with the transparency and experimentation of the management format. Initially, the management meetings focused officially on business issues only. The frequency was weekly, and the meetings were packed with agenda points. Gradually, as the culture developed (both across departments and in the leadership team), the teams became able to handle more and more business issues either locally themselves or with minimal support from the leaders. This meant that the management meetings changed in content and context. Fewer business issues were discussed, and those that were discussed did not include or affect all the leaders. The efficiency declined. This led to a redesign of the management meetings, which were split into two meetings, in alternating weeks. One focused on the rhythm of business while the other focused on the rhythm of connections.

Similarly, Pingala (a Danish IT consultancy with a progressive, modern organizational structure) has embraced the two rhythm components in its weekly meetings. Its strategic focus for many years has solely been culture, which has enabled the organization to move beyond the rhythm of business and to embrace the rhythm of connections too. Every week everybody gathers to have their town hall meeting, on Thursdays in the organization's Dubai office and on Fridays in the Danish office. The meeting agenda is focused on both aspects of rhythm, but with clear prioritization: purpose, people, progress and profit.

NETWORK BETWEEN TEAMS AND INDIVIDUALS

Network, relationships and ecosystem

How might we question:

How might we create and exploit the network between people, and between teams? How can we establish the kind of ecosystem that facilitates dialogue and connects people, teams and business entities, *and* can withstand and absorb a shock?

Recall the second of the four observations:

> **Teal Dots observation number 2:**
>
> Work happens in highly connected networks

The benefits of a networked organization (in contrast to a hierarchical organization) are manifold. They include:
- Faster access to experts and expertise
- A higher degree of fellowship and connection with the culture
- A higher degree of information spread
- Better use of the diversity in the organization to create stronger team cultures and better business solutions
- Understanding of the organizational dynamics, the innovation hotspots, the collaboration mechanisms and the influencers
- And, just as important in a disruptive business world, the ability to withstand and absorb shock

Jon Husband (2015) is a prominent advocate for the networked organization, calling it 'wirearchy' as a replacement for 'hierarchy'. As described by Sujin Jang (2017), knowledge about an organization's internal network is vital to cross-organizational performance.

Modern organizations consist of teams in a network. The approach to the mechanisms of the ecosystem falls in two parts: first, mapping and understanding the network and, second, exploiting and developing the network.

MAPPING AND UNDERSTANDING THE NETWORK

It is necessary to have a method of mapping the organization's internal network on a regular basis. This kind of investigation is called an 'organizational network analysis', and modern organizations perform this mapping once a year to understand the overall dynamics of the organization, to create a framework for debating team collaboration, and to spot and support the personal development needs of employees who are vital to the network.

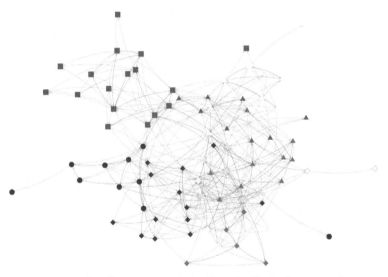

An example of an organizational network analysis, used to map internal relationships and understand an ecosystem.

Such mapping and investigations serve as mechanisms for understanding and exploiting the network for dialogue, problem-solving, inspiration and relationship-building, and several organizations use them as KPIs relating to their social capital.

See Part Four for more information.

EXPLOITING AND DEVELOPING THE NETWORK

The purpose of the network is to strengthen dialogue, increase the speed at which trust and fellowship grow, increase the level of tactical and operational execution, and create an ecosystem that can absorb shocks.

To do all this, it is necessary to develop cultural brokers – people who know people. People who know the culture and how the business works, and how they themselves work. People who act as bridges and adhesives between people and between teams.

Sujin Jang (2018) describes these cultural brokers as "team members who have relatively more multicultural experience than others and who act as a bridge between their monocultural teammates."

Jang's research has found that "cultural brokerage is a key factor that allows multicultural teams to capitalize on the benefits of diversity while mitigating the pitfalls. I define cultural brokerage as the act of facilitating interactions across parties from different cultural backgrounds." In studies, Jang has found that teams were significantly more creative when they had one or more members who acted as cultural brokers (Jang, 2017).

In a modern organization, how might we create and exploit the network between people and between teams? How do we establish the kind of ecosystem that facilitates dialogue and connects people, teams and business entities, *and* can withstand and absorb a shock?

The answer starts somewhere else – namely, with culture and fellowship. Building and nurturing the ecosystem starts with an interest and willingness to relate to each other, to be part of the culture and identity, and to be part of co-operative fellowships.

There is a correlation between organizational maturity and how employees come together as teams and networks.

The more modern the organization, the more cross-functional work is reported. The more time and effort the management team put into cultural work and team collaboration, the more social capital and psychological safety are created. These trends are not correlated with the size of the company or the impact of the work, but are correlated with the forward-thinking-ness and the amount of cultural work that takes place in the organization.

Again, this is a leadership task: to engage and commit yourself, your peers and your colleagues to each other. To strive to see the world through others' eyes. To facilitate and organize cross-silo dialogues. To bring people together. To establish the ecosystem.

EVALUATING YOUR LEADERSHIP AND ORGANIZATION USING THE NINE ELEMENTS

The role of the organizational fabric – the Orange World – is not to optimize for productivity and hierarchical distribution of responsibility and reporting, but to provide the right amount of support and nutrition to allow for spontaneous or guided emergence of self-governed and self-managed teams – the Teal Dots.

Your leadership task is to ensure that these nine elements are in place:

The nine elements of the organization of the future.

Evaluate the state of each of the nine elements in your organization. You can do this by yourself or with your leadership team, or let your employees do it. Use the schema below.

Make an intention for how you want to start and the direction you want to take. Vocalize it. Tell your leadership team and your organization that you want to develop yourself and the organization in this direction to create a new way of working with a different approach to the organizational platform and to self-managed delivery teams.

Create a controlled experiment with validated learning in a small area of your organization. Learn fast and scale fast. Reflect often. And keep in mind the four observations:

- Getting extraordinary things done in the modern corporate world happens in small teams only
- Work happens in highly connected networks
- Tactical execution happens when touchpoints are frequent and physical
- The reorganization as an activity is a pivot point for transformational leadership

	Today (currently): On a scale from 1 to 3, how mature is your Orange World?	Two years from now (intention): On a scale from 1 to 3, how mature is your Orange World?	What difference will this element make for you?	What do you need to strengthen to get there?
1. Purposeful organization, as a platform				
2. Culture and fellowship				

3. Individual coaching and stewardship				
4. Distributed leadership and decision-making				
5. Self-managed delivery teams				
6. Advisory boards				
7. White space mastery				
8. Rhythms in and across teams, networks and organization				
9. Networks between teams and individuals				
Total level of maturity (add the numbers together):			n/a	n/a

The main design thinking internally for culture
and leadership was the same as the externally
worded mission:

To empower every person and every organization
on the planet to achieve more.

The growth mindset approach is the exponent
and approach for this.
And we're all trained through this way of thinking.

———

Camilla Hillerup,
HR Lead, Microsoft Denmark

**Purposeful organization,
as a platform**

CHAPTER 6.

CASE STUDY: MICROSOFT DENMARK

– REDESIGNING THE APPROACH TO WORK FROM THE TOP DOWN AND INSIDE OUT

Company characteristics	
Company name	**Microsoft Denmark, with approximately 1,000 employees**
Industry	Microsoft produces computer software and hardware, consumer electronics, social networking services, cloud computing and video games.
	It is most famous for the Microsoft Office suite, the Microsoft Windows operating systems, Azure, Xbox and acquiring LinkedIn.
	Additionally, it provides professional services and consultancy to organizations, helping them to embrace the Microsoft product suite.
Company size	Approximately 140,000 employees worldwide, of which 1,000 are in Microsoft Denmark.
	Revenue in 2018 was $110 billion (€98 billion). Microsoft was ranked number 30 in the 2018 Fortune 500 rankings of the largest US corporations by total revenue.
Global presence	Microsoft is present in more than 120 countries worldwide.
Teal Dots in an Orange World profile	With the transformation that Microsoft Denmark has undergone in the past four to five years, it is safe to say that Microsoft Denmark is a Teal Dot in an otherwise Orange business world – and, inside the company, Teal Dots exist on top of a modern Orange World.

Microsoft has undergone tremendous development over the past five years, reinventing itself (again) as a modern company with a contemporary and forward-looking approach to leadership, company culture, and the development of employees and managers.

As stated on the Microsoft website, Bill Gates and Paul Allen founded Microsoft in 1975, and soon thereafter, they gave Microsoft a clear mission: "A computer on every desk and in every home." This was an extremely ambitious and visionary way of thinking and visualizing the kind of future that Gates and Allen wanted to create and foresaw. Over the next 40 years, Microsoft grew to be one of the leading technology companies globally, with more than 140,000 employees, offices in over 120 countries and $110 billion (€98 billion) in revenue in 2018. Clearly, this did not come without challenges and ups and downs, but nonetheless this is a successful company.

However, at times, rumour had it that the management style was somewhat performance oriented, playbook driven and KPI focused, with silos for local optimization of production and services. The management style that was suitable for the previous century needed an update – and Microsoft knew that themselves.

In 2014, Satya Nadella was named Chief Executive Officer for Microsoft, and in 2015 he revealed a new mission for the company: "Empower every person and every organization on the planet to achieve more."

This change in mission is the crux of the transformation. The change in mission from products to transactions is a beautiful framing of the new way of working, in which Microsoft wanted to support its users in achieving more through their work. Additionally, that wording captured a pivotal change that took place in the inner workings, mechanisms and culture in Microsoft. "Empower every person and every organization on the planet to achieve more," was targeted at Microsoft's employees as well as the market.

Naturally, Nadella and the new mission did not make it happen alone, with a magical snap of the fingers. Massive investment internally and a redesign of mechanisms were needed. It is a great example of what top-down leadership and change management are capable of creating, when thought about, designed and executed correctly.

MINDSET AND APPROACH

I met with the HR Lead of Microsoft Denmark, Camilla Hillerup, in their new offices in Lyngby, Copenhagen, built with the new way of working in mind: open spaces, daylight almost everywhere, task-based seating, concentration zones, etc. The offices have all the perks that you can imagine from a modern company, and – to some critics – the kinds of perks that are superficial and do not serve the real purpose of providing engagement and retention.

However, what Camilla Hillerup showed me about the inner workings of a reinvented Microsoft was fully in line with the physical impression of the building.

A look inside the modern offices of Microsoft Denmark.

Hillerup said, "We left the performance management and the playbook-driven approach behind. The core of the development was the wish to continuously be relevant to the market and to the employees – and to put a reframed purpose into our work. The new mission framed and phrased it perfectly."

Carol Dweck's (2007) approach to the growth mindset was instilled at the very centre of the company's approach to employees and leadership in general. In an interview in 2012 (OneDublin.org, 2012), Dweck explained:

> In a fixed mindset, students believe their basic abilities, their intelligence, their talents are just fixed traits. They have a certain amount and that's that, and then their goal becomes to look smart all the time and never look dumb.
>
> In a growth mindset, students understand that their talents and abilities can be developed through effort, good teaching

and persistence. They don't necessarily think everyone's the same or anyone can be Einstein, but they believe everyone can get smarter if they work at it.

Microsoft developed three focus areas for its application of the growth mindset to the organization and its pivotal development: customer obsession, one Microsoft, and diversity and inclusion.

These led to the development of three leadership principles that all managers and employees would be trained and mentored in: create clarity, generate energy and deliver success.

Grown mindset areas	Leadership principles
Customer obsession One Microsoft Diversity and inclusion	Create clarity Generate energy Deliver success

As Hillerup put it: "The main design thinking internally for culture and leadership was the same as the externally worded mission: to empower every person and every organization on the planet to achieve more. The growth mindset approach is the exponent and approach for this. And we're all trained through this way of thinking."

MECHANISMS AND TOOLING

Through this process of change, several vital elements shifted to have new mechanisms. Leadership became focused on facilitation, not on making business decisions. It became transactional, not product oriented. It changed to a focus on impact, not output. This in turn led to an updated mechanism for evaluating managers, namely contribution-based reflection and incentives, where the manager's personal performance KPIs are augmented with evaluation of their ability to grow and help others to grow: a person is a great manager if they contribute to others' success, build on others' ideas *and* reach their personal KPIs.

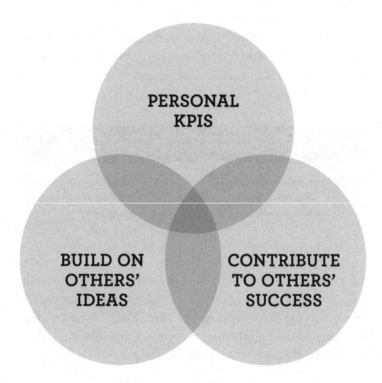

Microsoft's new mechanisms for evaluating managers, in line with the purpose of Microsoft and the philosophy of the growth mindset.

In summer 2017, a new element in this line of changes was embraced in the Danish branch, namely augmenting the matrix organisation in the sales and marketing business unit. A mix of communities of practice, virtual teams and networked organization emerged from two sides, bottom-up and top-down at the same time, with the purpose of focusing on customers and impact.

"All this hit rather hard here in Copenhagen," Hillerup explained energetically, "and we had a year of fumbling until we got the grasp of it. We replaced more than 20% of middle management, and of the rest, 80% were shuffled to new teams, where they performed and prospered much better. However, massive positive effects emerged in the wake of the changes."

Camilla Hillerup, HR Lead, Microsoft Denmark.

All 50 middle managers in Denmark went through a development programme and were lifted to new levels in terms of their skills, mechanisms and mindsets. At this offsite seminar, the managers were encouraged to draw their perceived internal network – that is, to create their personal organizational network analysis based on whom they talked to. Learning circles and debrief groups (each containing four managers) were formed across the organization to continuously nudge the managers to learn, share and contribute to each other's growth. And, throughout this period, the managers' development – both regarding their skills and their emotional journey – was visualized using the classic change curve, to give support to each manager and to give them a language with which to formulate their experiences and perspectives on the development.

In the less hierarchical structure, people started to form new internal dependencies and relationships. New interfaces and processes were revealed, built and strengthened internally between departments, experts and shared services. The existing rhythm of business was augmented with a rhythm of connections, focusing more on people's contributions to grow each other than on delivery of products and sales figures.

Now, the recruitment strategy focuses more on inclusion skills than cognitive skills. The search for talent is augmented with a search for potential. Data from MyAnalytics, Delve and LinkedIn are used to spot high-performing teams and to understand what makes them good, so the lessons can be shared. Analysis to predict employee retention risks is emerging. Talent assessments are handled by the whole management group to both help each other and enable people to learn.

The culture that has emerged is one of collaborative learning. Training and obtaining certificates are done together, in the teams and communities of practice, via blended learning, on-the-job-training and 'learning days' in which all 1,000 employees of Microsoft Denmark participate.

RESULTS AND THE FUTURE

Five major factors have shaped the path to where Microsoft Denmark is now:

1. The new CEO, Satya Nadella, and the new mission: "Empower every person and every organization on the planet to achieve more"
2. Embracing Carol Dweck's growth mindset and applying it to three areas: customer obsession, one Microsoft, and diversity and inclusion
3. Formulating new leadership principles: create clarity, generate energy and deliver success
4. Changing to contribution-based incentives, with a focus on contributing to others' success and building on others' ideas while achieving personal KPIs
5. Replacing the hierarchy and matrix organisation in the sales and marketing business unit with a network-based approach

This has been a massive, pivotal change, with several reframing twists. It took a year of fumbling in Denmark, but the results are strong.

Following over the page is an overview of the shifts and slides in the development of Microsoft Denmark over the past five years.

Perspective	New ways of working
A computer on every desk and in every home	Empower every person and every organization on the planet to achieve more
Fixed mindset	Growth mindset
Performance management	Contribution-based incentives
Playbook-driven approach	Leadership principles
Cascade communication	Rhythm of business Rhythm of connections
Do the things right	Do the right things
Award good performance	Award good contribution
Leadership decides	Leadership facilitates
Hierarchy and matrix	Platform of support Interfaces and relationships
Feedback	Perspective
Cognitive skills and talent	Inclusion skills and potential

This is clearly a modern approach to the Orange World that creates and shapes the organization, and in which teams can emerge, are supported and can be self-managed Teal Dots.

Camilla Hillerup glowed with passion and pride throughout our talk. I now understand why.

A year ago I participated in a lot of steering
committee meetings, and made a lot of
decisions on behalf of the teams.

Now, decisions are made in the teams
(in the Agile Release Trains and in the Scrum teams),
and now I spend my time with the business unit
leaders, understanding their business and
their challenges.

———

Michael Biermann,
CIO, Ørsted

Network, relationships, and ecosystem

CHAPTER 7.

CASE STUDY: ØRSTED

– BUILDING CROSS-ORGANIZATIONAL INTERFACES WITH NEW WAYS OF WORKING

Company characteristics	
Company name	**Ørsted A/S** Focus for the case study is the cross-organizational collaboration and interfaces between IT and the other business units, and the effort invested in building agile mechanisms in IT in order to create new ways of working.
Industry	The Ørsted vision is a world that runs entirely on green energy. Ørsted develops, constructs and operates offshore and onshore wind farms, bioenergy plants, and innovative waste-to-energy solutions and provides smart energy products to its customers. The three major business units in Ørsted collaborate with the IT Business Unit on more than 50 IT projects constantly, providing their colleagues in the business units and the group functions with IT operation, project management, and business advisory.
Company size	Headquartered in Denmark, Ørsted employs 6,200 people (2019). In 2018, the group's revenue was $12 billion (€10.7 billion). The IT business unit employs approximately 800 employees, in several global locations.

Global presence	Denmark, Poland, Malaysia, USA, UK and more.
Teal Dots in an Orange World profile	Ørsted IT is striving to build an approach to nurture self-managed teams that collaborate with the business units in a flat, networked approach. They focus on leadership, culture, and mechanisms for creating a platform for the teams; a modern Orange World that the Teal teams can live in.

Note: This is not a public statement from Ørsted. What follows is my perception and interpretation of their approach and learning from studying Ørsted for several years as employee and as advisor, and through interviews. Ørsted does not use the terms Orange and Teal themselves, nor such a deliberate approach.

Ørsted as a company has undergone a massive and pivotal transformation over the past decade. This has clearly required new ways of collaborating internally and across organizational structures. Agility and timely delivery of best practice-technologies, including IT services, has more and more become a unique selling point and a differentiator on the market; something that you win or lose customers and contracts on. This has required Ørsted to rethink the service delivery, the culture, and the collaboration approach across the business units and to establish a new approach to the internal ecosystem of employees and leaders.

DONG A/S (in 2017 renamed to Ørsted A/S) was founded as a national-owned company in Denmark as a result of the energy crisis in 1973, with the task to ensure independent delivery of oil and gas to the Danish citizens and businesses. Over the last decades, the company has been part of driving the energy transformation towards more independent, sustainable and green energy: so-called black energy resources are being phased out and gradually being replaced with sustainable resources like wind power, solar power, and biomass. In 2017, the name was changed to Ørsted, paying homage to the Danish scientist Hans Christian Ørsted (1777-1851) who discovered and described large parts of the behaviour of electromagnetism.

During this period, several pivotal changes and shifts have affected the development in the organization and the culture:

- The business shift in technology from oil and gas to sustainable delivery systems have created new demands for new engineering and IT technologies.
- The massive expansion in employees both due to mergers and acquisitions and organic growth have created new demands for the understanding of leadership, culture, and impact in the society.
- The local presence has shifted to a global one, regarding business locations and offices, regarding market presence and customers, and regarding energy trade across borders.
- And lately, a shift in cross-business unit collaboration has changed the way shared services and group functions work and identify themselves in a large conglomerate of different stakeholders.

Clearly, there is an opportunity and requirement to pivot the way collaboration and teamwork is handled, by adjusting the design and approach to leadership, culture, and distributed decision-making.

The previous understanding of transactional inter-company trade between business units is gradually being augmented – or even replaced – with a servant leadership approach to supporting each other. This is a massive change and Ørsted understands this. It takes time and it will never end in a state of 'done'. However, in a modern business world with shifts in identity, focus on impact and sustainability in organizations, millennial mindset, and fast and pivotal changes, this is the right way to address it.

In my opinion, zooming in on the collaboration between the business units and IT in Ørsted shows a brilliant case of how to create a modern Orange Platform, that the Teal-like teams (in various stages of maturity, health, and success) can emerge, form, live, deliver and disappear again. My interpretation of Ørsted's approach is that the Ørsted IT business unit is addressing two aspects at the same time: One, establishing a mechanism for the Teal Dots, and two, establishing an ecosystem with the business units that are in massive need for the IT services.

Ørsted's offshore wind farm at Anholt, Denmark

MINDSET AND APPROACH

In the 2000's and far into the 2010's, the collaboration between business units and the group functions in many corporate organizations was that of transactions and internal company trade.

Many Line-of-Business managers acted like they ordered software from a kiosk, or from a service catalogue. "I want ..." and "when can you deliver ..."

And likewise, many managers from IT or other group functions said things like: "I can deliver whatever you want, as long as you know what you want, and have the funding for it."

This kind of thinking might fit well in a best-practice oriented business world, on the rear edge of the dot com bubble and in the aftermath of the financial crisis. The approach at that time, especially to new technology and IT, was low risk and predictability. But with the VUCA world really kicking in, and the massive focus on changes in technology and society, time was changing.

Corporate collaboration in general was beginning to embrace new ways of working to handle risk taking and new technology in a faster and more experimenting way, and Ørsted was part of the movement, beginning to experiment with new ways of working like Scrum and Agile. This was driven by spearheads in both IT and the business units, having the will, courage and stamina to create a different and modern approach to IT services, prioritization mechanisms and cross-organizational collaboration.

Pia Verdich, Head of LACE (Lean-Agile Center of Excellence) in Ørsted IT describes the situation in the end of the 2010s in Ørsted: "Clearly, there was a supply-and-demand-thinking between the business units," she describes, "but in the end of the 2010s we started doing things differently. The challenge was that we did not deliver fast enough, nor relevant enough."

163

Pia Verdich, Head of Lean-Agile Center of Excellence, Ørsted

In 2016, one of the more profiled initiatives paved the way, baptized 'Dungeons and Dragons', which was a stand-alone experiment of working with Agile and Scrum, cross-functionally, driven by one of the business units.

By 2017, Ørsted had several local agile initiatives with dedicated roles from the business units, an IT delivery organization with a large amount of Scrum teams and growing experience and interest in working and thinking agile. An agile project model was developed to support the significant number of individual projects with agile methods and structure.

However, the planning was still local, and "local suboptimization thrived through individual steering committees," Pia Verdich recalls. Gradually, the need for further alignment, transparency, business prioritization and collaboration rose, and in 2017 Ørsted IT embraced the SAFe methodology. The Lean-Agile Center of Excellence was formed by Group IT, headed by Pia Verdich. "It started with a hypothesis based on a rough idea of what the future could look like, but very quickly we gained traction, especially because of the clear value-based business prioritization, increased transparency and close cross-functional collaboration."

When writing this (Summer 2019), eight Agile Release Trains (ARTs) are formed, each with between three and 12 high-performing standing Scrum teams in them. They have nine-month roadmaps with three-month detailed plans. Each ART is aligned with a business value stream and is funded with double-digit million DKK budgets per year. And each ART have a Collaboration Board providing advisory, consisting of the CIO, CTO, Head of Agile Delivery, Head of Business Applications, Head of Business Relations, and the Business Owners from the Line of Business. The meeting is headed/facilitated by ART Leadership.

Ørsted is looking into making the shared service functions part of the fixed teams in the ART's, representing IT, Procurement, Sourcing, Legal, People and Development, Risk, Finance, and other relevant Subject Matter Experts. In addition to that, Ørsted have so far formed ten Communities of Practice, where employees strengthen their shared professional skills and share learnings.

"Clearly," Pia Verdich states, "we are in the middle of an intense change journey, and it takes time to stabilize and mature the organization. However, results speak for themselves and we keep focus on creating a modern way of delivering digital products. We have ongoing commitment and release of capacity and funding. We are synchronizing intake on business requirements and releases in three-month rhythms across the business units. We have co-created an environment where we can adjust and embrace changes when they come."

The ambitions continue. Next wave will have focus on how to strengthen the lean-agile mindset. On employee development and the relationship between the leader and the employee. "We want to inspire – and to start a movement. We want to create a dialogue around the modern workplace based on empowerment, innovation and trust," Pia Verdich says.

This is supported with a three-pillar approach to what they call their Digital DNA: Agile, Design Thinking, and Change Management are the vital components in their Future of Work. Susanne Bork Klussmann, Senior Director and Head of Agile Delivery in Ørsted, describes the modern approach to business culture and the fusion of business and IT: "A significant part of modern business culture comes from the need for digitalization and collaboration. IT is a cultural medium for how to do business. We want IT to be a key enabler for the digital future of Ørsted. Culture, skillset and mindset are vital to this."

To support this, a Digital Academy with courses and programs is being launched, supporting especially the leadership and collaboration skills and mechanisms, that are needed for that kind of thinking, both in the teams and, just as important, between the teams and across the organization. The human interface mechanisms in collaboration and prioritizing effort, focus on user centricity and fast adaptation of the right products needs an update.

This transformation to teams and collaboration has caused a substantial change in what role and behaviour the leaders have. Michael Biermann, CIO for Ørsted, describes it rather colourfully: "A year ago I participated in a lot of steering committee meetings, and made a lot of decisions on behalf of the teams. Now, decisions are made in the teams (in the Agile Release Trains and in the Scrum teams), and now I spend my time with the business unit leaders, understanding their business and their challenges."

It is my interpretation of Ørsted's choices that they have managed to create a platform for a New Way of Working agilely, where it is not about transactions, but transcendence. It is not "can you deliver this to me?" but "can we solve this problem together?" They have redesigned their Orange World and made it possible for Teal Dots to appear and work together.

MECHANISMS AND TOOLING

What follows is a list of mechanisms, that Ørsted use to run their Agile setup.

Organizational design: Establishment of a culture of agility, with SAFe and Agile Release Trains, and Scrum teams. Creation of an Agile PMO, and a few new governance mechanisms for handling synchronization and funding, to ensure that they work on the right things in the right order. Establishment of Communities of Practice, and training in agile leadership and culture. Establishment of Advisory Boards, or committees for supporting the ARTs.

Leadership: A development in roles and behaviour from decision-making and local teaming, to relationship builder and business understanding. Massive focus on cross-organizational understanding and joint prioritization. Deliberate approach to distributing leadership and mandate to the teams, via mechanisms, behaviour, governance and values. The cultural work is immensely important in this.

Team membership and coaching: A part of designing the teams is keeping the team cross-functional and below nine members, preferably seven. Daily handling of conflicts, feedback and wellbeing is managed by the team as a team effort. If the team is unable to handle this, the Scrum Master takes over.

Maturity of the self-managed teams: Quarterly, an Agile Culture Survey is executed, creating a heatmap of the maturity of the teams. It focuses on six aspects, namely Level of 1) Empowerment, 2) Continuous learning, 3) Access to customers, 4) Fun at work, 5) Time for innovation and 6) Impact that matters. The ART employees answer the survey anonymously. The output is used in each specific ART as a part of their retrospectives, and by the Lean-Agile Center of Excellence to derive important learnings – to support and develop the teams.

Culture: Massive focus on behaviour and values, and on aligning them across the business units, the ART's, the teams, and the employees and leaders. "Inspirational Impact" is the mantra for the cultural work, and the leaders and Subject Matter Experts are role models in this. An Agile Leadership handbook is made, describing behaviour and 12 competences that goes well with the mindset of the agile leadership. Adding to that, the Digital DNA consisting of the three pillars of Agile, Design Thinking, and Change Management is positioned as the mindset and cultural fabric, supported by the Digital Academy with classroom training and online resources.

Communication: Naturally, as part of the Scrum sprint, regular touchpoints and retrospectives are performed both in the teams and across the ARTs. Microsoft Yammer is used heavily in and across the teams, supplied with the classic use of Outlook. Skype is used for video chat, and all documents are available for all via SharePoint.

RESULTS AND THE FUTURE

It is my observation, that Ørsted is building a new and fresh Orange World for their Teal Dots when it comes to IT services and development across the organization. Changing a large department with several hundreds of employees and managers into a platform for small teams to emerge is immensely difficult. It will never happen without mistakes, setbacks and frustration, but the leadership team insists on the direction.

To me, building the Orange Platform for their agile teams seems to be a profound and trustworthy way forward. The internal ecosystem is vital to a genuine dialogue and collaboration. The organizational work is handled where the tasks and challenges are, from the outside in. The teams are vital. The employees are supported in their individual development. And the leaders are redefining their role and work to be growth oriented and focused on paving the way for the teams.

Ørsted believe wholeheartedly, that in order to support their vision of a planet that runs entirely on green energy they need to collaborate, be agile, and engage their employees the best possible way in their work. The leaders take care of the employees, who then take care of the business. That is the ambition.

Our approach is to create the most
awesome company; a place we want to be
in for the rest of our lives.

Our time horizon is lifelong: in every moment
we create something that lasts forever.
And continuously we debate what the
right direction is.

Our culture *is* our product.

———————

Kent Højlund,
CEO, Pingala A/S

Culture and fellowship

PART THREE:
NEW WAYS OF LEADING

Part One: New ways of thinking	★ Four observations for the future to come
	★ Introducing the terms 'Teal Dots' and 'Orange World'
Part Two: New ways of working	★ Framing the right question; and the right answer
	★ Introducing the nine elements for the future organization
Part Three: New ways of leading	Gathering findings and discussions
	The paradigm shift: From leading people to leading ecosystems
Part Four: Practices and mechanisms	★ Showcasing real-life examples and approaches

This part gathers the findings from working with the four observations and the nine elements for building the modern Orange World. It describes the ecosystem, the paradigm shift in leadership that is needed and the organizational change management that fits with it.

CHAPTER 8.

THE PARADIGM SHIFT:

LEADING ECOSYSTEMS

For at least four decades, the approach to management and leadership has undergone massive development, and a paradigm shift in leadership towards 'leading people' has been ongoing.

Now, the modern organization is shifting from a hierarchical structure to a **sustainable ecosystem**. The modern Orange Platform with its Teal Dots has precisely such characteristics: a community of living organisms in conjunction with the non-living components of their environment, interacting as a system. With the birth of the idea of more self-managed or autonomous teams, a new approach to leadership has seen the light of day: we are evolving from 'leading people' to 'leading ecosystems'. This is your responsibility.

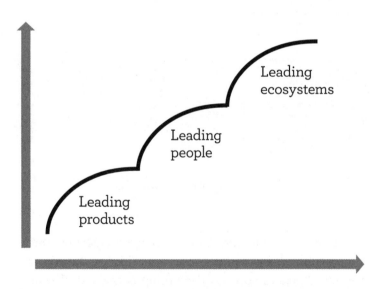

'Leading ecosystems' is about building and enabling a sustainable community and culture, where teams and people can live and interact with each other.

THE DYNAMICS OF A MODERN ORGANIZATION IN CONSTANT MOTION

What does daily life in a modern organization look like? How do you practise your leadership when you're running an ecosystem instead of managing a hierarchical organization?

Let us recall the descriptions that Laloux (2015) himself gives of Orange and Teal.

Colour	Description	Guiding metaphor	Key breakthroughs	Current examples
Orange	Goal is to beat competition and to achieve profit and growth. Management by objectives (command and control over what, freedom over how).	Machine	Innovation Accountability Meritocracy	Multinational companies Investment banks Charter schools
Teal	Self-management replaces hierarchical pyramid. Organizations are seen as living entities, oriented towards realizing their potential.	Living organism	Self-management Wholeness Evolutionary purpose	A few pioneering organizations

Source: Adapted from Laloux (2015).

Running a command-and-control hierarchical organization is compared to running a machine, like clockwork with well-oiled gears and cogs. Everything is tailored, designed and fitted together, turning in unison.

Running an ecosystem is a fundamentally different task from running a classical, hierarchical organization. An ecosystem consists of many self-managed parts that flow to and from each other, bump into each other, grow or shrink organically, and are affected by the organizational surroundings and mechanisms. They move independently of each other in what looks like Brownian motion but with direction – autonomously but aligned towards a shared direction and a shared purpose. They collide with each other and move buoyantly in the fluid they float in.

The analogy to the organizational ecosystem is strong. The Teal Dots move because of the interactions with other Teal Dots and with the modern Orange Platform that they exist on. The better you can design and lead that Orange Platform, the better you can affect the direction of the Teal Dots – your teams and people.

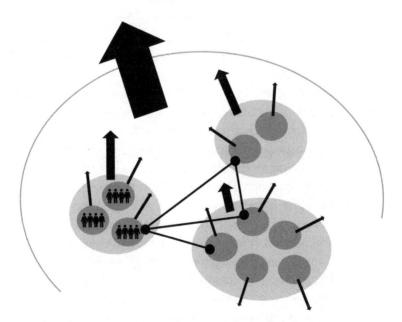

Autonomous teams, moving independently of each other, in an ecosystem. Some teams are aligned, some are not.

Running an ecosystem is about:

1. Understanding all the moving parts: both the teams and the people, and the mechanisms that make them move and interact
2. Maintaining an overview of the health and maturity of the moving parts and the surroundings
3. Nurturing and growing the parts and oiling the interactions
4. Infusing energy and nourishment
5. Removing the garbage, pollution and unwanted or poisonous elements

Translating this to our terminology, running the Teal Dots and Orange World ecosystem is about:

1. Having an overview of all the self-managed delivery teams and all of the nine elements in your organization – you must map them and understand their ways of working
2. Establishing a heat map of the maturity and cultural profile of all the teams, and a health map of all the mechanisms that you have or need
3. Establishing the required framework and actively engaging support for the life cycle of the Teal Dots and for constantly developing the mechanisms that are needed
4. Enabling information-sharing and dialogue, distributing tasks and projects, building the internal network and relationships, and establishing motivation, direction and acknowledgement of progress and results
5. Dismantling or dissolving teams and hierarchical structures that are no longer needed; removing pseudo-work, unnecessary bureaucracy and meaningless mechanisms that do not provide value; and eliminating poisonous culture and releasing employees who should be working for other organizations

Your role is to make the ecosystem healthy. Once you suc-ceed, the people and teams will flourish, naturally.

LEADING ECOSYSTEMS OF PEOPLE AND TEAMS IS A MULTIDISCIPLINARY TASK

A 'leading people' mindset encompasses principles such as people first; a constant search for purpose, meaningfulness and impact; willingness to experiment; a drive for results; and encouraging everybody to take part in the leadership. Whereas the old-fashioned 'leading products' approach is about transactions, 'leading people' is about transcendence.

Developing your leadership and yourself to master not only 'leading people' but also 'leading ecosystems' requires an expansion of your mindset. It needs holistic and soci-etal thinking, taking responsibility for not only people and teams but also the dynamic context and the interac-tions that the team and the people need and experience. It requires a new level of leadership skills and understanding, drawing upon new, multidisciplinary skills.

An ecosystem is dependent on flexible, movable components and a flow of information that allows (1) the components to interact with each other and (2) the components to develop and adjust to the context.

The mindset of 'leading ecosystems' embraces capabilities that enable the dynamics of the ecosystem.

This can only happen if the leader has mastered 'leading people'.

The modern, future-oriented leader focuses their time and attention on building the surroundings for the **teams**, and for their network and relationships.

A new business world requires a new way of leading. Deloitte described this approach to modern ecosystems, teams and team-based thinking in the 2019 edition of its *Global Human Capital Trends*, which states: "To tackle these challenges, organizations need to embed team-based thinking internally as well as in the broader ecosystem in which today's social enterprise finds itself. To help accomplish this, there are five layers in which team-based thinking should be embedded" (Deloitte 2019, p. 55).

Five layers of team-based thinking (Deloitte, 2019, p.55)

• **The ecosystem.** Define purpose-driven teams in the context of the missions they serve within the organization and externally relative to customers, partners, and society at large.

• **The organization.** Design 'front-led' networks of teams that promote multidisciplinary collaboration and empowered decision-making.

• **The team.** Build teams that demonstrate new agile and collaborative ways of working.

• **The leader.** Select and develop team leaders who have a growth mindset that creates the conditions for teams to be iterative, open, inclusive and effective.

• **The individual.** Challenge conventional talent management interventions, from succession and performance management to rewards and learning, to enable individuals to change their focus from climbing the ladder to growing from experience to experience.

There is no doubt that modern leadership in the modern organization is demanding and complex. Deloitte's report resonates with my own findings, including:

- Getting extraordinary things done in the modern corporate world happens in small teams only
- Work happens in highly connected networks
- Tactical execution happens when the touchpoints are frequent and physical
- The reorganization as an activity is a pivot point for transformational leadership

Leading ecosystems focuses on nurturing culture, organizational dynamics and building relationships, such that the employees themselves can get in the driver's seat for their engagement with and commitment to the projects and customers.

In addition to leading people, modern leaders lead the ecosystem that the people live in.

Leading ecosystems is the task of:
· Understanding the elements of the dynamic platform that the teams and people live in
· Identifying how to design and develop the elements, and in what priority
· Addressing the interfaces between those elements, between teams and between people
· Constantly fuelling and nurturing the dynamic stability of the ecosystem with energy, social capital, positivism, realism, ambition and humanism
· Ensuring that the ecosystem is sustainable

All this must be done while still having a 'people first' approach and an orientation towards the future of work.

The modern leader is a polymath – that is, their knowledge spans a significant number of subjects, they draw on complex bodies of knowledge to solve specific problems and they are masters of cross-pollinating those skills (Mikkelsen and Martin 2016).

The modern leader of ecosystems must master four capabilities, as shown in the following figure.

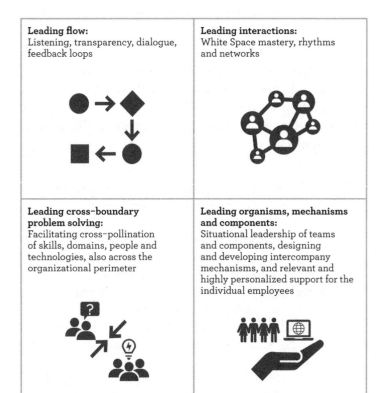

The capabilities of a modern leader of an ecosystem.

Leading flow: Mastering the art of listening, providing transparency to information and decisions, nurturing proper and genuine dialogue, and creating feedback loops for people and reflection.

Leading interactions: Mastering the white space, enabling and insisting on rhythms, and understanding and growing the networks inside and outside the organization.

Leading cross-boundary problem-solving: Facilitating cross-pollination of skills, domains, people and technologies, including across the organizational perimeter, to create better solutions and solve problems.

Leading organisms, mechanisms and components: Being able to identity and nurture the elements in the ecosystem. Applying situational leadership of teams and components, designing and developing intercompany mechanisms, and ensuring relevant and highly personalized support for the individual employees.

THE ECLECTIC LEADERSHIP OF
THE MODERN WORKPLACE

Eclecticism is a conceptual approach that draws upon multiple philosophies, ideas and theories when solving problems or addressing cases. An eclectic leader does not stand firmly on a single paradigm or set of practices, but applies wisdom to mix the relevant beliefs, assumptions and models, when needed.

As discussed previously, each team and collaboration unit in the Orange World has its own structure, design and mechanisms. The Teal Dot terminology in this book is designed to embrace that, with an understanding of the nuances in self-management and situational leadership. Likewise, the level of maturity of the team creates a mottled landscape of different teams, different interactions and different needs for organizational services and support.

The modern leader is **responsive** and understands the nuances of their role and the complex Orange World they are building. They apply their leadership with situational care and finesse:

- They are ambitious and diligent when it comes to applying and activating virtues such as humanism, personal charity, self-respect and listening; 'people first' lies close to their heart
- They are a role model when it comes to curiosity, courage, reflecting, making decisions and taking responsivity for shaping the future for themselves, their organization, their colleagues, their children, society and the planet
- They are digitally savvy, or at least not afraid of trying new stuff
- They experiment often, make mistakes regularly and extract learning from those mistakes every time

- They are familiar with sustainability movements and frameworks such as the United Nations' Global Compact and 17 Sustainable Development Goals

Their multidisciplinary skills and ability to improvise make them able to drive the modern organization forward. **The eclectic leadership style is that of a responsive leader.** It is very much in line with the thinking of sociocracy, the intention of the *Agile Manifesto* (Agile Alliance, 2001), the build–measure–learn approach from lean startup, and the Teal spirit of living organisms, self-management, wholeness and evolutionary purpose.

The modern leader is Teal at heart, is responsive and is a leader of an ecosystem. Modern leadership is deeply rooted in sustainability and connectedness. No man is an island.

CHAPTER 9.
LEADING THE PARADIGM SHIFT

> Real change happens in personal behaviours,
> or at larger scale in entire organizations, only when
> we take time to discover this sense of what's worthy
> of our shared attention.
>
> Margaret J. Wheatley, *Leadership and the
> New Science: Discovering Order in a Chaotic World*
> (2006, p. 174)

Developing and evolving your organization from one that is characterized by hierarchy and old-school management to a modern Teal and Orange ecosystem is challenging and takes years.

Changes will be needed everywhere – in structures, processes and tools; in culture, language and virtues; in the interactions between people and between the organization and the teams; and in personal behaviour and how the employees perceive the organization.

PRACTICE MAKES BETTER

Clearly, leadership and change management in the modern world are immensely interwoven. Every action, decision, communication and behaviour is part of change management, whether by creating awareness, showing the way forward, or giving perspectives on other or better approaches to challenges.

Modern organizations are champions when it comes to handling changes, and unconsciously they are evolving their approach to change from 'change management' to 'change enablement': changes are not things that must be managed but things we enable.

It cannot be a surprise that those organizations that continuously change things (small or large) are the ones that can adapt to new trends, technologies or market conditions. Practice makes better. There are three reasons for this.

First, frequent changes makes it possible for the organization to constantly improve its mechanisms for change management – that is, how it investigates, experiments, rolls out and evaluates changes.

Second, the employees become more accustomed to changes and gradually adjust their emotional reactions to them.

Third, the changes – and especially the organizational redesign – are a perfect storm and opportunity for practising the intended mode of leadership with live feedback.

ORGANIZATIONAL SHOCKS, ANTIFRAGILITY AND SUSTAINABILITY

Be aware of the challenges of establishing and running Teal Dots and the Orange Platform. Two things are at stake here.

First, immature Teal Dots are fragile. They need constant engagement, reflection and willingness to succeed. Teal Dots need dynamic stability, and constant infusions of energy and attention. They are costly, some might say, as they do not run without supervision. However, once the Teal Dots reach a level of maturity where they become self-managed, they need remarkably less external energy and sponsorship, as they become self-regulating, which leads to self-management. This does not, however, imply that they are immortal and incapable of failure and meltdowns. Healthy Teal Dots are antifragile (Taleb, 2012) and have grit, but they still need attention. See also the section on advisory boards and situational leadership in chapter 5.

Second, spotting design mistakes in the Orange Plat-form can be hard to do. They can often be hidden or over-shadowed by areas that need attention or an otherwise harmless yet energy-demanding conflict. And, often when the design mistakes rise to the surface, they release a burst of suppressed energy and criticism.

Ecosystems can resist and absorb shocks. Structures cannot. For a structure to break down, a single root cause is enough. For an ecosystem to break down, many root causes are needed, as the ecosystem is inherently built for adaptation and absorbing changes. One root cause cannot break an ecosystem. When an ecosystem breaks, you'll find a multitude of symptoms and a multitude of root causes; each is insignificant and harmless but together they are devastating for the ecosystem's balance.

This can be handled only by creating feedback loops and frequent reflection points. The progressive organi-zations that are showcased in this book have weekly ret-rospective sessions and strive to handle feedback within hours. This makes their ecosystems better at handling changes and even organizational shocks. This makes their ecosystems sustainable.

REORGANIZATION IS AN OPPORTUNITY FOR CULTURAL DEVELOPMENT

The best implementation and adaptation of new ways of working happens when both the mechanisms and the leadership are applied simultaneously. This gives opportunities to practise, reflect, adjust, align and improve behaviour and the shared mindset.

Teal Dots observation number 4:

The reorganization as an activity is a pivot point for transformational leadership

---

Modern change management is characterized by controlled experiments, frequent feedback loops and agile adjustments. This is the exact same approach you should have to the reorganization of your organization – to the way that it develops and evolves. The goal is twofold: obviously to create the Orange Platform and the nine elements that it consists of, but also to affect and influence the employees' perception of the leadership and culture that you are striving to establish.

It is always the **perceived** leadership and culture that form the real yardstick for the impact of the leadership's activities.

Employees' experience of their organization is largely based on their **perception** of the leadership via the daily life of the organization – this is what matters to employees.

Jacob Morgan describes the employee experience as being based on "the long term redesign of the organization that puts people at the center" (Morgan, 2017). To him, the employee experience is made up of employees' perceptions of the cultural environment, the technological environment and the physical environment.

THE EMPLOYEE EXPERIENCE EQUATION

The employee experience equation, Morgan (2017).
Employee experience is the perception of the cultural
environment, the technological environment
and the physical environment.

Source: Jacob Morgan (thefutureorganization.com, 2015)

Building a modern Orange Platform in the right way – using the nine elements and thereby constructing an eco-system for your organization – will pave the way for exactly what Morgan describes above.

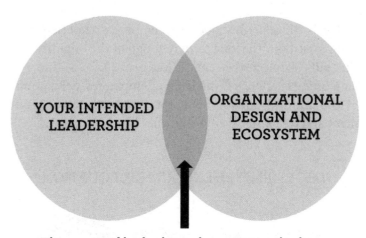

The **perceived** leadership and organizational culture:
The amount of alignment and coherence between the intended
leadership and the organizational design and ecosystem

In a VUCA business world, changes are hard to predict, plan, execute and finalize. Instead, small experiments and frequent learning create remarkable results. The keys to success are transparency, openness to input, ideation and asking questions. This holds for the massive organizational changes and reorganizations required, for changes in mechanisms on the Orange Platform, and for the leadership and culture you are striving to implement and propagate.

It is often said that the success of organizational change relies on mapping the organization's internal social capital and identifying the nodes of the organizational network; these are your change agents. This idea is supported by research documenting that strong relationships are key to both strategic activities and reorganizations. In a study with 884 respondents, Susan E. Lynch and Marie Louise Mors found that "[network] ties that are relationally embedded are less likely to be affected by change in the formal structure," and thus form the core of the organizational ecosystem (Lynch and Mors, 2019, from the abstract).

The more active, authentic and responsive the leadership you practice, the more alignment and overlap you will establish between your intended leadership and the organization design.

The more vocal and outspoken you are about your intentions, the better involvement and support you will get. As Margaret J. Wheatley (2006) said, change happens when we work for "what's worthy of our shared attention" (p. 174).

CHAPTER 10

CASE STUDY: THE MINDSET OF A MODERN LEADER

– KENT HØJLUND, CEO OF PINGALA A/S

Company characteristics	
Company name	**Pingala A/S**, founded 2008
Industry	IT consultancy in the enterprise resource planning (ERP), customer relationship management (CRM) and business intelligence (BI) domains, delivering Microsoft D365FO, CRM, and BI advice and solutions
Purpose	"An oasis for the market's most talented Dynamics 365FO, CRM and BI people for the benefit of our customers in a lifelong cooperation"
Company size	Over 50 employees and growing
Global presence	Two offices in Denmark, one in Dubai
Teal Dots in an Orange World profile	Pingala as a company is a full-blown Teal Dot in an otherwise Orange World around it, both in Denmark and in Dubai

Kent Højlund, CEO of Pingala A/S since 2013.
Source: Photo by Mark Knudsen, Monsun.

What is on the mind of a modern, Teal leader?

What drives a person who insists on creating an organization that he wants to work in himself for the rest of his professional career?

And what advice would he give to someone who is about to initiate the transformation themselves?

PINGALA:
A TEAL DOT IN AN ORANGE BUSINESS WORLD

Intuitively but unconsciously, the Danish company Pingala A/S has been using Teal mechanisms since it was established.

Indeed, this was a deliberate approach that paved the way for the organization, which has grown from two to now over 50 employees. The motivation was a genuine wish to create an organization and culture that were fundamentally different from the previous experiences that the founders had had. However, the Teal framework – or any of the SALT frameworks for that matter – was not the blueprint for their design. Pingala was featured as a case study in *The Responsive Leader* (Østergaard, 2018). The following is an excerpt from the full case study.

> Back in 2008 two Danes, Anders Nielsen and Henrik Berg Andersen, founded Pingala with the idea of creating a company they would want to work in for the rest of their professional careers. Both had personal experiences from long engagements with customers, delivering IT solutions to the ERP market. Both agreed on what they had learned from these engagements. They now wanted to create something that fitted them perfectly, for the rest of their lives. They wanted great teamwork, fruitful dialogue with customers, and a culture acting as a lever for relation-based collaboration. They wanted high expertise. They also wanted no oversold or derailed projects, and fair compensation and salary.

The mission for Pingala is to be "An oasis for the market's most talented Dynamics 365FO, CRM and BI people for the benefit of our customers in a lifelong cooperation." (As it was formulated in 2015.)

When Kent Højlund was engaged as CEO in 2013, he asked himself:

How can we firmly scale the company from 10 to 100 employees, AND stay true to the original idea of a company that we would want to work in for the rest of our professional careers, with a flat organization and no managers?

In what ways do we need to differentiate ourselves with regards to our ecosystem, our partners, our delivery mechanisms, and culture – both to attract the right talent, and to beat competition?

How can we create a
'Blue Ocean' in an otherwise Red Sea?

From Østergaard (2018, p. 271-272)

The CEO is the only person with a formal management role and title. Otherwise, Pingala is a fully flat organization with no managers. Employees have peer-to-peer mentoring and the internal relationships are measured yearly via an organizational network analysis.

Pingala has worked on its culture consistently over several years and treats its culture as its product. Over the past years, several modern mechanisms have been experimented with and embraced in Pingala to support and develop the organization, the relationships and the social capital.

And the results have been massive. Pingala has had exponential growth in terms of number of employees, number of customers, gross profit and bottom line, and has a consistently high customer satisfaction score. It has been awarded a *Børsen Gazelle* (given on the basis of impressive growth and revenue) for seven consecutive years. Still, the most important KPI for Pingala is the eagerness to show up for work – in other words, the will among its employees to create an oasis for themselves, in lifelong collaboration with their customers.

Pingala has been awarded a *Børsen Gazelle* for seven consecutive years.

Clearly, with the CEO being responsible for the organization, the employees, the strategy, the financial results and the culture, Kent Højlund plays a vital role in the nurturing and growth of Pingala, with the crucial support and collaboration of the founders, partners, board of directors and employees.

Let us put Kent Højlund, CEO of Pingala A/S, in the spotlight.

THE MINDSET OF A MODERN CEO

"It is not about control. It never is," Højlund said.

Højlund is a remarkable leader. He is the most patient CEO I have ever met when it comes to driving cultural development and activities. He has a rare psychological profile with high drive and massive emotional skills, a combination infrequently found among CEOs. His business acumen is rounded out by American software sales roles and experience in the IT world, augmented by a profound interest in areas such as appreciative inquiry and organizational psychology. The employees genuinely like him.

"I'm driven by the idea of building an organization I want to be part of for the rest of my life," Højlund said. "I want to lead the organization, but not lead the employees. I don't want to steer. I want to create the ability for the employees to steer, when needed."

When Højlund joined Pingala he had the intention to focus for a year on culture, then a year on sales, then a year on something else. However, with Pingala's special setup and group of employees, he quickly realized that his number-one priority and the strategic focus every year should be culture. Culture became the theme of all company-wide activities and workshops, which involve analysing and developing Pingalas skillset and mechanisms from any angle possible.

"Leading the organization is 90% culture. One of our most important processes is recruiting and onboarding of new employees. Finding the right employees is important," said Højlund.

One of the first things Højlund did was to launch a competitor analysis, which among other things involved systematically trawling through LinkedIn to count the number of management levels and non-billable employees at Pingala's competitors. Højlund explained: "Many organizations have a large or very large overhead in non-billable management layers or administrative functions. I found that 30-50% of the employees worked in non-billable positions. We wanted to avoid that. We wanted to create first-line empowerment. The individual employee should have the will and possibility to take end-to-end responsibility for their work and accountabilities, without three, four, five management layers between the real work and the real decisions."

To Højlund, a customer escalation is seen as an opportunity to strengthen the lifelong collaboration even further. "I focus on sparring with the customers' CXOs on a holistic level. I focus on communication, understanding and collaboration. Our employees and the customer's employees then focus on the task at hand and they become much better at handling the problems, once the cultural approach has been aligned between the organizations."

CREATING A MODERN CULTURE WITH MODERN MECHANISMS WITHOUT MANAGERS

Pingala wants to hire the best employees only. For Pingala, 'best' requires not only a focus on professional skills (general technology understanding, business affiliation and specialist knowledge) but also a focus on emotional intelligence, the ability to create and maintain relationships, likability and willingness to be part of nurturing the culture actively.

Creating a unique culture and a unique approach to customer engagement was Pingala's way of creating a Blue Ocean in an otherwise Red Sea (Kim and Mauborgne, 2015). Over the years, Pingala has established several mechanisms to support and develop both the organization and the individual employees. To mention a few:

- The weekly town hall meeting for all employees follows a structure with a focus on the most important area first: purpose, then people, then state of the union, then progress on projects and activities, and finally (and only once a month) profit and financials.
- The town hall meeting is opened with the following question to all: "What have you done or observed a colleague doing in the past week to support our mission?"
- The town hall is also used to share experiences with customers, both good and bad, and to share mistakes and learning.
- The most important weekly KPI is measured directly at the town hall meeting via the so-called Team Temperature, where every employee rates their own week on a scale from 1 to 6 and provides a comment on why they chose that specific rating.
- The annual employee conversation and one-to-one dialogues with managers have been removed, because there are no managers to handle such meetings.

Since Pingala wants to grow from 10 to 100 employees with a flat organization, the CEO simply cannot find the time to handle individual conversations with everyone. Instead, each employee has a peer-to-peer mentor board composed of employees who have been pinpointed as close and significant to that employee in the annual organizational network analysis. In that way, every employee gets a mentor who is relevant to them, either professionally or socially.

- Employees are empowered to choose their projects and customers themselves. No one forces them to engage in activities. When customers hear about this, they see the culture as a massive opportunity for collaboration and quality.
- Internal work is orchestrated in circles – inspired by sociocracy and holacracy – focusing on culture, methodology, internal communication, etc.
- Six to eight times per year, they all gather for six-hour workshops on culture, interpersonal skills, trust, etc.

Building a modern organization without managers but with a large amount of self-management also affects the role of the board of directors (BOD), its members' approach to the strategic work and their support to Højlund. Often, a traditional BOD has a focus on growth and preparing the organization for financial performance, a merger or being acquired by someone.

"But this is not the goal for us, nor for the BOD," Højlund said. "We focus on the Oasis [a reference to Pingala's mission], on people's dreams and our wishes. The BOD must understand and support our culture. We do not need BOD members that are focused on cashing in or maximizing their profit. The BOD supports the idea of the Oasis, and creating lifelong engagement with the employees.

Financial growth is not a goal, but a tool to ensure organic, controlled organizational growth."

The purpose of the BOD is to enable Højlund to focus on the purpose of Pingala (on keeping people engaged) and to give him freedom. This approach is reflected in the agenda for the BOD meetings, with three regular points in prioritized order.

"The first point is always 'people and recruitment'. It's the most important for us and for the BOD. Then 'key figures vs. budget' and finally 'pipeline', followed by a few 'any other business' points," said Højlund.

The culture is the real product. They want to build an oasis for the market's most talented Dynamics 365FO, CRM and BI people for the benefit of their customers in lifelong co-operation. And they mean it.

HOW DO YOU INITIATE THE DEVELOPMENT?

Where should you start? Looking at the nine elements of the new way of working, Højlund immediately highlighted two of them:

- Purposeful organization, as a platform
- Culture and fellowship

"This is where you start. You have to have this in place," said Højlund. "Your purpose is vital. You need to know why you go to work, and what benefit it creates. Our culture is our product. This is why we're here, and why I go to work."

To Højlund, fellowship is an ingrained and integrated part of Pingala and its culture. It is about creating the oasis; the watering hole in a desert; a space with psychological safety, trust and strong relationships. "Our approach is to create the most awesome company – a place we want to be in for the rest of our lives. Our time horizon is lifelong:

in every moment we create something that lasts forever. And continuously we debate what the right direction is. Our culture *is* our product."

This kind of visionary ambition is symptomatic of Pingala and Højlund's thinking. To focus on the immediate moment in order to create something lifelong. To create psychological safety by not telling people what to do. To focus on operational excellence to ensure cultural leeway.

"It's so much easier to be patient when there are fewer rules and politics to navigate through, and no prestige in titles. However, we also expect high performance and operational excellence, both from ourselves and our colleagues. We're ambitious," said Højlund.

This is exactly what Kent Højlund is. Ambitious – and patient.

Mindset and culture are way more important
for us and for our hiring process.

We're looking for someone that fits in.

Growth mindset is important,
more than experience.

———————

Michael Bruun Ellegaard,
Chief Culture Officer,
Trustworks A/S

Culture and fellowship

SUMMARY AND CONCLUSION OF PARTS ONE TO THREE

Using the double-diamond approach from design thinking, we can summarize the findings and discussions of the book so far as follows.

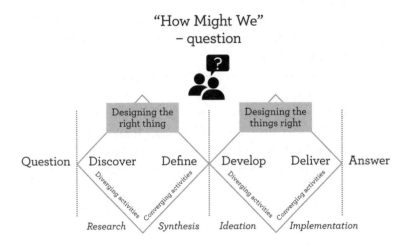

We know that the business world is changing, dramatically. We know that new ways of working are emerging, exemplified most prominently by SALT (sociocracy, agile, lean startup and Teal). We also know that these kinds of organizational models are hard – maybe almost impossible – to scale to large corporate organizations.

THE QUESTION

How might we design our organization so that it is resilient to change and human centric, and in such a way that we can handle the transformation in a manageable way as part of our daily life?

How might we create something where every employee experiences a Teal or agile-like culture, with mechanisms that are truly scalable?

My research has revealed four observations about future organizations:

- Getting extraordinary things done in the modern corporate world happens in small teams only
- Work happens in highly connected networks
- Tactical execution happens when the touchpoints are frequent and physical
- The reorganization as an activity is a pivot point for transformational leadership

This book's synthesis shows that we can take advantage of progressive organizational structures and create a platform that supplies them with the needed interactions:

- Create Teal Dots, not Teal everywhere
- Redesign the space between the Teal Dots – that is, redesign your Orange World
- Establish a hyper-connected network between the organizational gravitational points

The resulting 'how might we' question is: how might we design the elements and the dynamics that constitute an ecosystem for our organization? How might we design and lead the modern Orange World?

This book's ideation reveals nine elements of the future of the organization – nine elements that create the ecosystem:

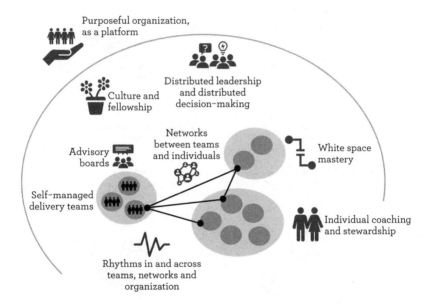

This book has also identified a new approach to leadership, namely **'leading ecosystems'** in addition to 'leading people':

Leading flow: Listening, transparency, dialogue, feedback loops	Leading interactions: White Space mastery, rhythms and networks
Leading cross-boundary problem solving: Facilitating cross-pollination of skills, domains, people and technologies, also across the organizational perimeter	**Leading organisms, mechanisms and components:** Situational leadership of teams and components, designing and developing intercompany mechanisms, and relevant and highly personalized support for the individual employees

THE ANSWER

Abandon the idea of teams working in a hierarchy. Instead, introduce the idea of several self-managed teams with their own aims, domains, members, ecosystems, rhythms and responsibilities. Apply Teal or sociocratic thinking to these circles, or Teal Dots. Teal Dots should be small, with a maximum of five to seven employees.

Create an ecosystem. Redesign the organizational support system to be one that acts as a platform that the Teal Dots spawn on, live on and evaporate from. This is your Orange World: a platform-way-of-working or organization-as-a-service to the Teal Dots. The organization serves the teams, not the other way around.

Teal Dots can work together as circles with neighbouring circles, in small Teal ecosystems. They might resemble flowers, with petals surrounding a central circle. The Teal flowers should be limited to, say, a maximum of five to seven Teal Dots.

Create a rhythm of frequent touchpoints for dialogue between the Teal Dots and the Teal flowers. Form advisory boards to each Teal flower, not for reporting but for support.

Nurture the internal network between employees who are subject matter experts, information brokers or social anchor points. Use it for feedback loops, for idea generation, for dialogue, and for access to experts and expertise. You might form professional communities of practice too.

Make sure that the group's functions are proactive, are part of the rhythm and take an interest in the touchpoints.

Expect the unexpected. Provoke the unexpected. Use your rhythm to react.

Develop your mindset, mechanisms and structure at the same time.

Create humane and sustainable leadership, based on connectedness.

THE IMPLEMENTATION

One last part of the double diamond is missing now. One crucial part, namely **the implementation**.

This is the part you must handle yourself. Use the build–measure–learn approach.

Remember:

Modern leaders strive to create organizations where they themselves want to show up, day after day.

The philosophy is humanistic, sustainable and based on the idea of connectedness:

No man is an island.

We choose to go to the Moon! ..
We choose to go to the Moon in this decade and
do the other things, not because they are easy, but
because they are hard; because that goal will serve
to organize and measure the best of our energies
and skills, because that challenge is one that we are
willing to accept, one we are unwilling to postpone,
and one we intend to win.

US President John F. Kennedy,
Houston, Texas, on 12 September 1962

**Purposeful organization,
as a platform**

PART FOUR:
PRACTICES AND MECHANISMS

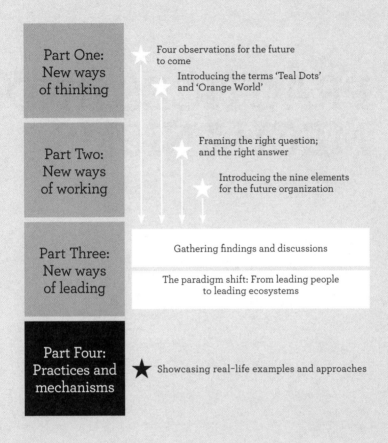

Part One: New ways of thinking	Four observations for the future to come
	Introducing the terms 'Teal Dots' and 'Orange World'
Part Two: New ways of working	Framing the right question; and the right answer
	Introducing the nine elements for the future organization
Part Three: New ways of leading	Gathering findings and discussions
	The paradigm shift: From leading people to leading ecosystems
Part Four: Practices and mechanisms	Showcasing real-life examples and approaches

This part showcases real-life approaches to building and maintaining the dynamics of modern organizations.

CHAPTER 11.
PRACTICES AND MECHANISMS

CHAPTER 11.
PRACTICES AND MECHANISMS

How do progressive organizations and modern leaders design their mechanisms? What are the good practices that they use and apply?

What follows are **real-life examples** of building and maintaining the dynamics of modern organization, each of them designed, tested, adjusted and used in practice.

They are presented not as tools with fully fledged process descriptions, preconditions, postconditions, roles and actors, and data flow, but as overall practices. The reason is to enable you to design your implementation yourself, using the build–measure–learn approach.

Start by take the temperature of your organization, together with your colleagues and employees:
- Benchmark how progressive your organization is by using the Maturity Assessment (see Chapter 3)
- Benchmark your Orange World by investigating its maturity
- Reflect on your own mastery of 'leading ecosystems'

Then: reflect on what mechanisms you must have to establish the nine elements of the organization of the future. Use the table on the next page as inspiration.

Element	What mechanisms do we have?	What mechanisms are we missing?
1. Purposeful organization, as a platform		
2. Culture and fellowship		
3. Individual coaching and stewardship		
4. Distributed leadership and distributed decision-making		
5. Self-managed delivery teams		
6. Advisory boards		
7. White space mastery		
8. Rhythms in and across teams, networks and organization		
9. Networks between teams and individuals		

Get inspiration from the following examples and real-life approaches to building and maintaining the dynamics of modern organizations.

PURPOSEFUL ORGANIZATION, AS A PLATFORM

The most important element and the crux of your organization is understanding why you are here. **Why does this organization exist? Why should anyone care?** Why do you go to work? You need to understand and convey your organization's purpose and what meaningful services and behaviour you strive to deliver and nurture.

DESCRIBE YOUR PURPOSE VIA IMPACT STORIES

A good purpose statement immediately answers these questions: Why does this organization exist? Why should anyone care? Why do you go to work?

Use this structure to create impact stories that describe what you do, for whom, and what they obtain from that:

> We [insert a verb, or a phrase with a verb]
> so that [insert a role]
> can [insert a goal or ability].

Start in the middle by understanding who you deliver your services to. Use the resulting impact story internally or externally, as you see fit. The approach is inspired by Simon Sinek (2009) and by user stories from the Scrum world (Sutherland, 2014).

ACTIVATE THE PURPOSE

Bring the purpose to life by actively using it for prioritizing, motivation, setting direction, measuring progress, celebrations and acknowledgements. Use it in presentations, to say yes and no to projects and tasks, for evaluation and feedback, and to create identity and understanding.

Example: start each regular status meeting or town hall meeting by asking, "Since we met the last time, what have we done to support our purpose?"

Describe the value you deliver to your customers by using the Value Proposition Canvas by Strategyzer (2019b).

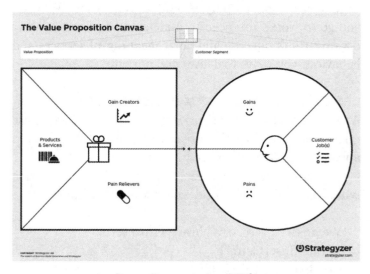

Source: Strategyzer.com (2019b)

IMPACT ACCOUNTING

Use the impact stories to describe the value or impact that you want to create. Agree on how you want to measure the impact, how often, and how you want to use the results.

1. Focus on the value you create
2. Describe its functional, emotional and societal value
3. Aim it at your stakeholder groups: your employees, your customers and society

4. Establish regular feedback loops for gathering data on the actual or perceived value – that is, measure the impact and your value creation
5. Debate the mutual understanding of activities and prioritizations
6. Adjust these activities adequately

Agree on how you want to publish the results. Only internally, or also externally on your webpage and as part of your annual report?

Describe your business model using the Business Model Canvas (Strategyzer, 2019a) to understand how value creation emerges and what components it entails, so that everybody understands end to end how the organization serves its customers.

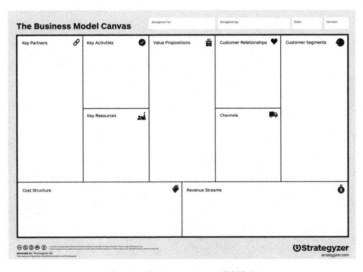

Source: Strategyzer.com (2019a)

REDESIGN YOUR CORPORATE FUNCTIONS:
THE MODERN BUREAUCRACY IN AN ORANGE WORLD

Redesign how the existing bureaucracy and corporate group functions should support the ecosystem of self-managed delivery teams, by:

1. Making a list (like the one opposite) of all the services that are present in your organization
2. Evaluating the need and shape of each service in the future
3. Redesign the services to be both on-demand and just-in-time services

Services present on the individual level	Services present on the corporate level	Services present on the outside
• Engagement and motivation • Daily coaching • Professional sparring • Conflict handling • Regular appraisal • Personal development plan	• Prioritization of business activities • Funding of business activities • Anchor budgeting • Identifying and distributing tasks and projects • Project portfolio review • Cascade dialogue • Rhythms of business • Rhythms of connections • Invoice handling • Purchasing • Salaries • Bonuses and incentive structures • Internal communication • People and culture services • Legal • Compliance and regulatory affairs • IT • Tax and VAT	• Corporate communication • Customer relationships • Sales activities • Marketing • Mergers and acquisitions • Cross-perimeter collaboration

Ensure that the group functions think and act as platform partners to the teams and employees. The mindset is that of a service provider and sparring partner, not a transactional product subcontractor. As inspiration, read *Transformational* HR by Perry Timms (2017).

CULTURE AND FELLOWSHIP
DESCRIBE YOUR CULTURE AND YOUR FELLOWSHIP
Organizational culture in the future of work is one of communities and belonging – that is, of co-operative fellowships. The things that shape and reflect your culture are behaviour, words, physical environment and your tools – and the emotional responses to those things.

Describe the behaviours that characterize you as an organization – those that create and shape your identity. Use the Culture Map by Strategyzer to facilitate the dialogue (Osterwalder, 2015).

Source: Strategyzer.com (Osterwalder, 2015)

DESCRIBE THE PERCEPTION OF THE CULTURE

Perception is reality. Use the PERMA model by Martin Seligman (2011) to gather examples of concrete situations for each element, to get an understanding of how your employees and peers perceive the culture and what experiences they have:

	Describe concrete examples of situations for each element. Be as specific as you can.
Positive emotion	
Engagement	
Relationships	
Meaning	
Accomplishments	

DESCRIBE GOOD PRACTICE – AND BAD PRACTICE
Describe what defines good practice and bad practice.
Use a scheme like this:

The ideal: We strive to ..	The compromise: Sometimes we have to ..	Below our standard: We never ..

TAKE THE TEAM'S TEMPERATURE WEEKLY
On a weekly basis, facilitate a process of reflection:
1. Send a small survey to your employees to let them answer the following questions:
   Looking back on this week, on a scale from 1 to 6:
   How happy are you with your relationships?
   How happy are you with your results?
   How happy are you with your workload?
2. Gather the results and publish them anonymously on a weekly basis.
3. Facilitate a round of reflection. Why was it a good week? Or a bad week? What should we keep doing – or try doing differently? Typically this takes a few minutes.

Aggregate and share the results in the circles or team of teams, or where relevant.

INDIVIDUAL COACHING AND STEWARDSHIP
ESTABLISH BUDDY RELATIONSHIPS,
CULTURAL BROKERS AND STEWARDSHIPS

Ensure that every employee gets a buddy or a steward who helps them to manoeuvre around the organization and tackle whatever challenges or opportunities arise. Onboarding is especially crucial in this.

NETWORK-BASED ONE-TO-ONES AND MENTORSHIP

Abolish the traditional, hierarchical hub-and-spoke one-to-ones, where the manager of a team takes turns speaking to each team member over a period of a month.

Instead, apply a networked approach and establish peer-to-peer mentoring, where the people coach and mentor each other in small groups of three. You could use the results from an organizational network analysis to establish mentor–mentee pairs, where the mentor is a person that the mentee has referred to as a good relationship, either professional or social. A third employee, a relevant colleague, can be appointed based on daily work with the mentee.

The point is to establish a culture of coaching on peer-to-peer level, which is way more situational and contextual than any manager would be able to provide.

MODERN ONE-TO-ONE CONVERSATIONS

Modern one-to-one conversations have gradually come to focus more on how the employee is feeling rather than their tasks at hand. The key question is 'How are you?' instead of 'What are you working on?'.

Use the team's temperature (see opposite page) as input.

You could also use Daniel Pink's (2009) model for motivation as a tool for dialogue, with the added element of psychological safety.

- Psychological safety
  - › How are your relationships with your colleagues? Do you work well together? Do you have fun together?
  - › Do you feel that you can ask questions, be sceptical and express that you are uncertain?
  - › Do you experience relevant, timely feedback?
  - › Do you know how your colleagues assess your performance?
- Autonomy
  - › Do you have enough influence on what tasks you're working on?
  - › Do you have enough influence on how you handle them?
  - › Are you okay with your degree of manoeuvrability?
  - › Do you have the relevant mandate to make decisions?
  - › Can you manage your own time?
- Mastery
  - › Do you have the right skills to master your current tasks?
  - › Do you have any unused skills?
  - › Do you get the right support from your colleagues and managers?
  - › Do you have enough experience? Or too much experience?
  - › Are the tasks right for you?
  - › Do you have enough time to handle the tasks to the expected quality?
- Purpose
  - › Do you know the purpose of the organization? Is it meaningful to you?
  - › Do you know what value your current project provides to our customers?
  - › Do your daily tasks make sense to you?

PERSONAL EVALUATION BASED ON
A GROWTH MINDSET

Establish contribution-based reflection and incentives that show people's ability to grow and help others to grow. For example, somebody is a great employee if they:

1. Contribute to others' success
2. Build on their colleagues' ideas
3. Take responsibility for their own growth
4. Reach their personal goals

DISTRIBUTED LEADERSHIP AND DISTRIBUTED DECISION-MAKING

USE THE FULL SPECTRUM OF LEVELS OF DELEGATION TO GET A SHARED AGREEMENT

Use this five-level approach – inspired by Delegation Poker by Management 3.0 (2019) – to agree on the level of delegation between a leader and an employee, or the advisory board and the team.

**Leader /
Advisory Board**

I make the decision

You give advice;
I make the decision

We make the decision
together

I give my advice; you
make the decision

You make the decision

**Employee /
Team**

Establish **overall agreement** on functional areas such as hiring, salary and value propositions, and make on-the-spot and **contextual agreements** when needed.

DECISION-MAKING IN TEAMS OR GROUPS

Establish mechanisms for group-based decision-making. Investigate the various approaches to decision-making. Agree on the right approach in the context. Corporate Rebels (2019) has created a helpful overview of the different approaches and their characteristics:

- Autocratic
- Consensus
- Democratic
- Consent
- Delegation

Sociocracy uses consent-based decision-making: "A (facilitated) group process for decision-making: invite objections, and consider information and knowledge revealed to further evolve proposals or existing agreements" (Sociocracy 3.0, 2019).

Holacracy uses integrative decision-making (Robertson, 2016): present a proposal, invite clarifying questions, initiate a reaction round, amend and clarify, initiate an objection round, and integrate objections. See also Holacracy.org.

DOCUMENT YOUR DELEGATION AND AGREEMENTS

For the **overall agreements**, create a delegation board that shows the levels of delegation and autonomy for each area.

For the **contextual agreements**, I propose an adjusted RACI template: the REDI template:

	Who	Our agreement on delegation
Responsible		
Executing		
Dialogue		
Information		

SELF-MANAGED DELIVERY TEAMS
GATHERING TEAMS: SIZE MATTERS
In the modern organization, teams will be small. Team size will drop to approximately five to seven employees, due to interaction fatigue: ingrained characteristics of the modern team are frequent dialogue and stronger relationships. The larger the team, the more relationship ties to maintain and information channels to use.

TEAMS THAT INTERACT

Teams can work together as circles with neighbouring circles, in small ecosystems. They might resemble flowers, with petals surrounding a central team. The ecosystems should be limited to, say, a maximum of five to seven Teal Dots.

Do not think of the teams as being in a hierarchical reference system but address them with equal justification.

DEFINING THE FRAMEWORK FOR YOUR TEAMS:
THE TEAM CHARTER

A self-managed team should have a team charter that describes three things: expectations of each other, agreements, and rhythm for evaluation and adjustment. The team charter should answer these questions:

Why: What problem are we solving? What opportunity are we exploiting? What meaning are we creating, for whom? What identity are we creating with our shared purpose?

What: What meaningful goals are we seeking? What meaningful value are we creating? When will the problem be solved? What is the expected output? What is the expected outcome? When will we be done? And what is the definition of done?

Who: Who are we? Are we the right people to solve the problem? Do we have the right competencies? Do we have the necessary time and bandwidth to be part of the team? Do we really want to join in and be part of the team, and solve the problem? Do we understand each other's individual personal styles and ways of working? Do we have proper relationships with each other? Who are our stakeholders, partners, vendors and other collaborators? Who are our change management agents and influencers? Who are the people and departments that our work will impact?

How: How do we plan to get there? What is the shared plan for our work? What are the activities and their dependencies?

What is our mandate? How much freedom do we want to have? And how much do we get in reality? How do we measure progress (both on output and outcome) and make sure that we are on the right path to solving the right problem?

RHYTHM OF TEAMS

Debate and agree on a rhythm for reflection on and evaluation of the behaviour and virtues of your team. In contrast to the establishment and formulation of the questions above, the operationalization of the answers is not at all something you can address bit by bit in a formula. Instead, it requires a mindset and approach that address these challenges:

- How can we ensure that we do the right things right?
- How can we create shared values and norms?
- How can we create shared and mutual responsibility?
- How can we create frequent and useful feedback?
- How can we create energy and engagement?

The solution is to create a rhythm in your team with a higher frequency than in the old days, and with psychological safety to discuss relationships and results.

RHYTHM OF TEAMS THAT INTERACT WITH OTHER TEAMS

Rhythm is crucial to the wellbeing and progress of a team, and of teams that interact:

- Hold daily co-ordination meetings, including across teams that interact
- Hold weekly or bi-weekly demonstration meetings, focused on delivery
- Hold weekly or bi-weekly reflection meetings, focused on collaboration and culture

ADVISORY BOARDS

GATHERING ADVISORY BOARDS

The best-functioning advisory boards consist of two, or a maximum of three, experienced employees from the organization who have business understanding, interpersonal and humanistic skills, and enough technical and project management insight to provide advice and sparring.

THE ROLE OF THE ADVISORY BOARD

The role of the advisory board is to provide the right amount of advice, input, coaching, support and instruction to the teams, based on their maturity and the situation they are in. This is highly contextual and dynamic and should be assessed and adjusted regularly. You might use the levels of delegation to get a mutual understanding of the role and responsibility.

The advisory board should meet with the team on a bi-weekly basis – no less and not 'when we need it'. Rhythm and steadiness are important, as they will have the side effect of supporting white space mastery.

THE SITUATIONAL LEADERSHIP OF THE ADVISORY BOARD

The advisory board's closeness to the team and the types of activities it engages in with the team will depend on the maturity of the team. Use the so-called Pizza Model to investigate the team's roles and competencies in four areas (Østergaard, 2018):

Business orientation

Business understanding
Value chain, R&D,
production, sales, marketing,
internal organization,
external stakeholders and
actors, compliance, market
understanding, support
processes, understanding
the customers processes etc.

Delivery orientation

Making things happen
Facilitation, project
management, meeting
deadlines, budgeting,
analysis, estimation,
building, testing, analysis,
documentation etc.

People orientation

Interpersonal skills
Leadership, mentoring,
coaching, motivation,
empathy, conflict handling,
emotional intelligence etc

Specialist orientation

Professionalism
Coding, chemistry,
engineering, photography,
nursery, management etc.

The Pizza Model of roles and competencies in a team.

241

For each slice of the pizza, ask:
- Does the team have the competencies that are needed?
- Does the team have overlap or gaps?
- What development areas are there, either areas that are crucial to the success of the team or learning opportunities driven by the wishes of the team members?
- Is the team in a state of learning or doing, or is it even capable of teaching other teams?

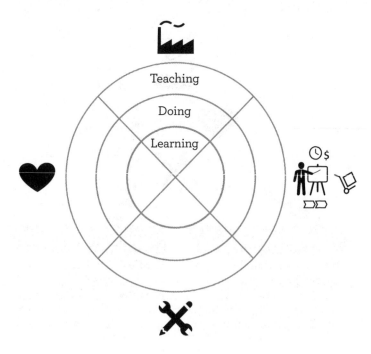

Based on this investigation, the advisory board should shape its situational leadership approach to fit the maturity of the team:

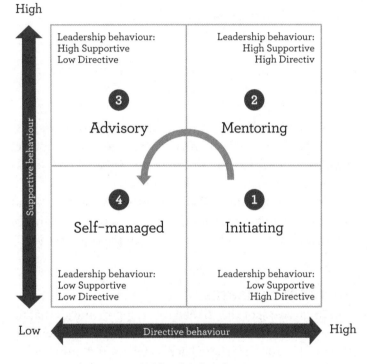

High

Supportive behaviour

Leadership behaviour:
High Supportive
Low Directive

3
Advisory

Leadership behaviour:
High Supportive
High Directiv

2
Mentoring

4
Self-managed

Leadership behaviour:
Low Supportive
Low Directive

1
Initiating

Leadership behaviour:
Low Supportive
High Directive

Low

Directive behaviour

High

Situational leadership for teams.

Source: Adapted from Hersey and Blanchard (1969) to focus on supporting the development and maturity of Teal Dots in an Orange World.

GIVING ADVICE

Just like a coach or mentor, the advisory board should be excellent at asking questions such as:

- Have you considered...?
- What will happen if...?
- What is your approach to...?
- Who have you involved in...?

USE THE MATURITY ASSESSMENT TO MAP THE CULTURE IN THE TEAM – AND TO MAKE A HEAT MAP OF THE ORGANIZATION

As described previously, you can use the Maturity Assessment (see Chapter 3) to investigate and map the level of maturity in the team, in the team of teams and across the organization.

Use it to understand the differences in the teams and thus the need for leadership support from the Orange World, and from the advisory boards in the organization.

WHITE SPACE MASTERY

How might we spot the challenges or opportunities that no one has seen yet? How do we ensure that relevant experiences and lessons are shared across teams and units?

WORKING OUT LOUD – IN PUBLIC

A culture of working out loud where all employees take part in sharing their work, their challenges and their problem-solving approaches will gradually enable employees to handle white space. They will chip in with good advice or learning. They will spot information that can be used elsewhere or that can cross-pollinate with their solution. They will spot trends or share external information that others can use in their work.

The classic town hall meeting should be redesigned. It is often boring, because it feels irrelevant and one way. Managers tend to use cascade communication. Instead, we need dialogue – for example, in smaller groups or via an electronic platform for voting, giving feedback or asking questions.

The tedious 'let's take a round where everybody shares what they are working with' process must have a twist. Make sure not to merely share your activity but also focus on what you have learned, mistakes you have made, problems you need help with or exciting things that you want to work with. Chances are that your colleagues will find interest or relevance in what you say, take part in the knowledge-sharing and join forces to collaborate.

WORKING OUT LOUD – ONLINE

Online collaboration tools such as Microsoft Teams or Slack are excellent places to practice #WorkingOutLoud.

Share where you are each morning with a picture and a 'Good morning, colleagues' update. Use hashtags to make your updates discoverable in themes. Ask questions. Answer questions.

Modern knowledge management is not a task of knowing where things are but knowing who knows. It's a task of relationship-building and white space mastery.

INFORMATION LIAISON OFFICERS

Often organizations have a few naturally skilled white space ninjas per 100 employees. These employees close the gaps between the teams and employees unconsciously without knowing it. They have an intuitive humanistic approach to engaging with people, strong listening skills and a high level of emotional intelligence, and they are very familiar with codifying group dynamics and body language. They also have either strong business understanding or technological savvy.

During their daily interactions with colleagues or teams, you'll often hear them say things like 'Well, team ABC had the same challenge – they did...', 'I think you should talk to X and see if she should be part of your debate' or 'I felt the customer was a little indecisive – maybe X should show him their solution again.'

These informal liaison officers often have broad and widespread roles in their organization – typically as subject matter experts, resource managers, competency anchors or similar. They work with multiple tasks and projects and have massive interfaces in the organization.

If you are not one yourself, you should spot them. They are worth their weight in gold.

RHYTHMS IN AND ACROSS TEAMS, NETWORKS AND ORGANIZATION

Running a business depends heavily on a healthy and steady approach to managing alignment.

In modern organizations, alignment is ensured by facilitating rhythms for both of the following:

- A mechanism for the synchronization of business activities between the teams for which collaboration and alignment are important, right now
- A mechanism for developing teams, growing employees, and in general developing the wellbeing and health of the organization

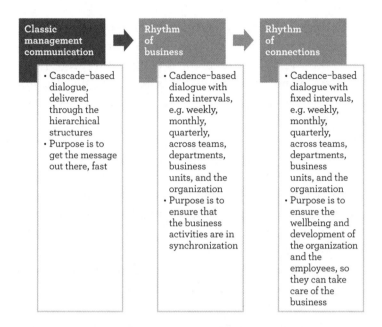

PRACTICES FOR THE RHYTHM OF BUSINESS

The best practice embraces rhythm-based dialogue with fixed intervals, e.g. weekly, monthly or quarterly, across teams, departments, business units and the organization. The purpose is to ensure that the business' activities are in synchronization, taking care of the value chain, key processes, and quality governance, to deliver your services and processes.

Highly inspired by Scrum and Scaled Agile Framework, the idea of the rhythm of business comes from daily standups, working in two- to four-week sprints, and PI (programme increment) planning across teams and in Agile Release Trains. This aligns smoothly with a modern approach to strategy planning on an enterprise level. See, for example, the case study of Ørsted in Chapter 7.

Strategic and tactical execution is handled in megasprints of three- or six-months duration. Just as with Agile/Scrum, the content and activities of the next upcoming megasprint are aligned and agreed upon just-in-time, and adjustments are handled either as part of the local rhythms or when the megasprint ends.

PRACTICES FOR THE RHYTHM OF CONNECTIONS

The modern organization is seen as a community, not as a production machine. The focus is on people, recruitment, team temperatures, wellbeing, feedback loops and the dynamics of the network. The approach is that of a growth mindset:

- How can we help people succeed?
- Which teams are performing well, and why?
- Which teams need support?
- What skills and capabilities do we need?
- How does the organization's social capital look?
- Do the employees experience psychological safety?
- What should we do to strengthen engagement and empowerment?

It is good practice to have:

- Daily meetings in production teams
- Weekly team meetings to reflect on collaboration and wellbeing
- Weekly or bi-weekly department meetings with a focus on culture
- Bi-weekly leadership meetings with a focus on culture, employees, talent management, recruitment, etc.

See, for example, the case study of Microsoft Denmark in Chapter 6.

WEEKLY TOWN HALL MEETINGS FOCUSING ON CULTURE, PEOPLE AND RELATIONSHIPS

There should be a one-hour Friday meeting with a focus primarily on connections and secondarily on business. The agenda should be based on the four Ps of modern leadership: purpose, people, progress and profit.

Purpose: What have we done since last time that supports our purpose?

People: Who is new to the team? Who is leaving the team? And how are we feeling? Take the team temperature.

Progress: What is going on in the business, in the market, with the customers, with the projects, and with the services and deliverables?

Profit: News on financials and KPIs.

The order of the agenda points is important.

LEARNING DAYS EVERY SIX WEEKS

A good practice seen at Pingala (see the case study on Kent Højlund, CEO of Pingala, in Chapter 7) is to have six-hour learning days every six weeks focused solely on people, culture, collaboration and relationships.

These are supplemented with in-between activities focused on developing both cultural mechanisms and production mechanisms, with reports back delivered at the weekly town hall meetings and the learning days.

BROAD ALIGNMENT OF TASKS AND ACTIVITIES, AND SHARING OF EXPERIENCES

It can be highly beneficial to gather the team leads, resource managers, key account managers, marketing managers, product owners and technical architects all in one room every week for a two-hour meeting to distribute tasks and activities to teams.

This serves the need for business progress and the need to ensure that any dependencies and risks will surface quickly enough to be handled.

DISTRIBUTION OF INFORMATION

The monthly or quarterly town hall meeting is a well-integrated institution in the modern organization, where all employees are invited to a one-hour or three-hour gathering to share information.

Interestingly, this approach is being complemented with in-between online information-sharing mechanisms. Following are a few that are being used in large Danish organizations:

- A daily two-minute Skype morning meeting, where the top leaders brief the organization on what is going on after their own morning meeting in their confidential briefing room (this is seen in a very dynamic, high-risk financial institution in Denmark)
- A weekly 15-minute Skype meeting where the leader briefs the business unit about news and activities
- A bi-weekly 10-minute video recorded by the CEO to share his view on the 'state of the nation'
- Using Snapchat to distribute small information videos to a younger crowd of workers (15-17 years) with daily updates on processes and with small personal (and funny) greetings

NETWORKS BETWEEN TEAMS AND INDIVIDUALS

MAPPING THE INTERNAL NETWORK AND UNDERSTAND THE SOCIAL CAPITAL

It is necessary to have a method of mapping the internal network on a regular basis. This kind of investigation is called an 'organizational network analysis', and modern organizations perform this mapping once a year to understand the overall dynamics of the organization, to create a framework for debating team collaboration, and to spot and support the personal development needs of employees who are vital to the network.

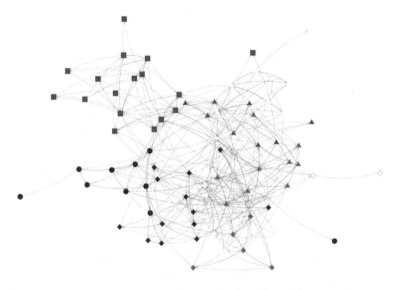

An example of an organizational network analysis, used to map internal relationships and understand an ecosystem.

One of three approaches is usually used to perform these mappings.

First, using data from communication platforms and systems in the organization to map dialogue paths (data from email, instant messaging, collaboration platforms, document management systems, etc.). This is the most controversial method, as it feels like surveillance and sneaking a look at data. However, it is already in use today at places, in a light and accepted format.

Second, asking employees who they work with, who they use for professional sparring, who they get energy from and who they talk with about things that are unrelated to work. This approach is the most commonly used and relies on direct reflections from employees. The illustration above was created using this approach.

Third, mapping what questions that are asked in the organization, who's asking and who's answering. Qvest, a Danish organization, provides a service that enables organizations to do exactly that: to map the flow of questions in an organization. Prominent thinkers such as Hal Gregersen are promoting this kind of curiosity in organizations: encourage people to ask the right questions. "Questions are the answer," states Gregersen (2018).

STRENGTHENING RELATIONSHIPS
Use an organizational network analysis to find and activate:
- The cultural ambassadors
- The information hubs
- The social bridges and gravitational points
- Clusters of strongly connected employees

Encourage those people who are nodes and connectors to strengthen relationships. Engage them as connection points between people and between teams. Use them as keynote speakers at learning days, interview them for your internal podcast, engage them in change management initiatives, bring them together as sounding boards in the organization, etc.

Other ways to develop networks include setting up 'speed dates' or 'lunch dates' between colleagues or teams, have 'follow a colleague'-days, introduce a routine of interviews between employees leading to a small article on the intranet, etc.

Arrange lunch meetings across the business units. Establish team building. Hold training in cross-cultural understanding. Spend time describing your team and culture to your colleagues. Break habits and choose another desk in an open space – or in the canteen. Speak up when you have knowledge that others might be interested in hearing.

Encourage cross-organizational collaboration. Create teams that are unusual and driven by diversity. Sit somewhere that you do not usually sit.

CHAPTER 12.
GET STARTED

So, how to get started? Get inspired by the case studies of Trustworks (Chapter 3) and Pingala (Chapter 10), which showcase how fully flat organizations work and what kind of leadership is needed. Look at the case studies of Microsoft Denmark (Chapter 6) and Ørsted (Chapter 7), which illustrate how the organizational platform for collaboration and teamwork can be dramatically developed.

You should also regularly take the temperature of your organization, together with your colleagues and employees:

- Benchmark how progressive your organization is by using the Maturity Assessment (see Chapter 3)
- Benchmark your Orange World by investigating its maturity
- Reflect on your own mastery of leading ecosystems

BUILD

- Involve your organization. Let the employees come up with ideas for taking the organization to the next step. Use the nine elements as a blueprint for your organization and the ecosystem
- Plan a way forward: establish some experiments that will provide you with data and insights, both on mechanisms and interactions, and from people

MEASURE

- Gather data and insights from your experiments often and openly
- Ask your employees how they feel

LEARN

- Show and debate the findings, and the feelings and experiences
- Reflect. Adjust. Learn. Celebrate. Repeat.

After five to six months, benchmark yourself again.

By doing this you will be able to embrace the constantly changing business world and create an organization that is adaptable and relevant to the market and to its employees – and a place where you want to show up for work yourself too!

THIS IS HOW TO ORGANIZE
THE WORKPLACE OF THE FUTURE.

REFERENCES

ADP Research Institute. *The Global Study of Engagement: Technical Report.* ADP Research Institute, 2019. Accessed 17 September 2019. https://www.adp.com/resources/articles-and-insights/articles/g/global-study-of-engagement-technical-report.aspx.

Agile Alliance. *The Agile Manifesto.* Agile Alliance, 2001. Accessed 17 September 2019. http://agilemanifesto.org.

Albæk, Morten. *Ét liv, én tid, ét menneske.* Copenhagen: Gyldendal, 2018.

Bøtter, Jacob. *Forget Your IQ: Think about Your NQ.* Copenhagen: Heute Denken Morgen Fertig, 2012.

Buckingham, Marcus, and Ashley Goodall. "The Power of Hidden Teams." *Harvard Business Review.* Last modified 20 May 2019. https://hbr.org/cover-story/2019/05/the-power-of-hidden-teams.

Bughin, Jacques, Eric Hazan, Susan Lund, Peter Dahlström, Anna Wiesinger and Amresh Subramaniam. *Skill Shift: Automation and the Future of the Workforce.* McKinsey Global Institute, 2018. Accessed 17 September 2019. https://www.mckinsey.com/featured-insights/future-of-work/skill-shift-automation-and-the-future-of-the-workforce.

Center for Ledelse. *CfL-Undersøgelser om nye organisationsformer.* Center for Ledelse, 2019. https://www.cfl.dk/viden/indikatorer/cfl-undersoegelser-nye-organisationsformer.

Christensen, Clayton M. *The Innovator's Dilemma: The Revolutionary Book that Will Change the Way You Do Business.* New York: Harvard Business Essentials, 1997.

Corporate Rebels. "Bad Decisions Make Good Stories."
Last modified 3 January 2019.
https://corporate-rebels.com/decision-making-processes.

Corporate Rebels. "The 8 Habits of Companies You Wish You Worked for
(and How to Put Them into Practice)." Last modified 19 April 2017.
https://corporate-rebels.com/the-8-habits.

Corporate Rebels. "How to Disrupt a 70,000 Employee Manufacturing
Company." Last modified 30 January 2019.
https://corporate-rebels.com/disrupting-haier.

Deloitte. *The new organisation: Different by design: 2016 Deloitte
Global Human Capital Trends*. Deloitte University Press, 2016.
Accessed 19 September 2019.
https://www2.deloitte.com/content/dam/Deloitte/bm/
Documents/human-capital/trinidad/2016%20HC%20Trends_
TrinidadCountryReport.pdf.

Deloitte. *Rewriting the Rules for the Digital Age: 2017 Deloitte
Global Human Capital Trends*. Deloitte University Press, 2017.
Accessed 17 September 2019.
https://www2.deloitte.com/content/dam/Deloitte/global/
Documents/About-Deloitte/central-europe/ce-global-human-
capital-trends.pdf.

Deloitte. *The rise of the social enterprise: 2018 Deloitte Global
Human Capital Trends*. Deloitte University Press, 2018.
Accessed 19 September 2019.
https://www2.deloitte.com/content/dam/insights/us/articles/
HCTrends2018/2018-HCtrends_Rise-of-the-social-enterprise.pdf

Deloitte. *Leading the Social Enterprise: Reinvent with a Human Focus
– 2019 Deloitte Global Human Capital Trends*. Deloitte University
Press, 2019. Accessed 17 September 2019.
https://www2.deloitte.com/content/dam/insights/us/
articles/5136_HC-Trends-2019/DI_HC-Trends-2019.pdf.

Dunbar, Robin. *Grooming, Gossip, and the Evolution of Language*.
Cambridge, Mass.: Harvard University Press, 1998.

Dweck, Carol S. *Mindset: The New Psychology of Success*. New York:
Ballantine Books, 2007.

Falkenberg, Puk. *Knowledge Creation in a Knowledge-Intensive Firm:
How to Conceptualize Tacit Knowledge in a Change Management
SME*. Thesis. Slagelse: University of Southern Denmark, 2016.

Gallup. *How Millennials Want to Work and Live*. Gallup, 2016.
Accessed 17 September 2019.
https://www.gallup.com/workplace/238073/millennials-work-live.aspx.

Gregersen, Hal. *Questions Are the Answer: A Breakthrough Approach to Your Most Vexing Problems at Work and in Life*. New York: HarperBusiness, 2018.

Hamel, Gary. *Reinventing the Technology of Human Accomplishment*. University of Phoenix Distinguished Guest Video Lecture Series, 2011. Accessed 17 September 2019.
https://www.youtube.com/watch?v=aodjgkv65MM.

Hersey, Paul, and Kenneth H. Blanchard. *Management of Organizational Behavior: Utilizing Human Resources*. Jersey City: Prentice Hall, 1969.

Husband, Jon. *Wirearchy*. Montréal, Québec: Wirearchy Commons, 2015.

Ismail, Salim, Michael S. Malone, Yuri van Geest and Peter H. Diamandis. *Exponential Organizations: Why New Organizations Are Ten Times Better, Faster, and Cheaper than Yours (and What to Do about It)*. New York: Diversion Books, 2014.

Jang, Sujin. "The Most Creative Teams Have a Specific Type of Cultural Diversity." *Harvard Business Review*. Last modified 24 July 2018. https://hbr.org/2018/07/the-most-creative-teams-have-a-specific-type-of-cultural-diversity.

Jang, Sujin. 2017. "Cultural Brokerage and Creative Performance in Multicultural Teams." *Organization Science*, November-December: 993-1009.

Kim, W. Chan, and Renée Mauborgne. *Blue Ocean Strategy, Expanded Edition: How to Create Uncontested Market Space and Make the Competition Irrelevant*. Boston, Mass.: Harvard Business Review Press, 2015.

Kniberg, Henrik. *Spotify Engineering Culture (part 1)*, 2014. Accessed 19 September 2019
https://blog.crisp.se/2014/03/27/henrikkniberg/spotify-engineering-culture-part-1

Kolind, Lars, and Jacob Bøtter. *UNBOSS*. Copenhagen: Jyllands-Postens Forlag, 2012.

Krautwald, Alexandra. *Unge generationer på arbejde*. Copenhagen: Dansk Psykologisk Forlag, 2018.

Küblböck, Manuel. 2019. "Why We Treat Employees Like Adults
– and the Trade-Offs This Entails." Last modified 27 April 2019.
https://medium.com/the-caring-network-company/why-we-treat-
employees-like-adults-94f50fbe9cd.

Laloux, Frédéric. *Reinventing Organizations: A Guide to Creating
Organizations Inspired by the Next Stage in Human Consciousness.*
Brussels: Nelson Parker, 2014.

Laloux, Frédéric. "The Future of Management Is Teal."
strategy+business. Last modified 6 July 2015.
https://www.strategy-business.com/article/00344?gko=30876.

Lederne. *Digitalisering og ny teknologi: Betydningen for lederrollen.*
Copenhagen: Lederne, 2018.

Lynch, Susan E., and Marie Louise Mors. "Strategy Implementation
and Organizational Change: How Formal Reorganization Affects
Professional Networks." *Long Range Planning* 52, no. 2 (2019): 255-270.

Management 3.0. "Delegation Poker & Delegation Board."
Last modified 26 March 2015.
https://management30.com/practice/delegation-poker.

Mikkelsen, Kenneth, and Richard Martin. *The Neo-generalist:
Where You Go Is Who You Are.* London: LID Publishing, 2016.

Minzberg, Henry, Joseph B. Lampel, James Brian Quinn and Sumantra
Ghoshal. *The Strategy Process: Concepts, Contexts, Cases.* Englewood
Cliffs: Prentice-Hall, 1988.

Morgan, Jacob. "The Complete Guide to the 5 Types of
Organizational Structures for the Future of Work."
The Future Organization. Last modified 23 July 2015.
https://thefutureorganization.com/the-complete-guide-to-the-
5-types-of-organizational-structures-for-the-future-of-work.

Morgan, Jacob. *The Employee Experience Advantage.* New York:
John Wiley & Sons, 2017.

OneDublin.org. "Stanford University's Carol Dweck on the Growth
Mindset and Education." Last modified 2015.
https://onedublin.org/2012/06/19/stanford-universitys-
carol-dweck-on-the-growth-mindset-and-education.

Ørsted, Christian. *Livsfarlig Ledelse.* Copenhagen, Denmark:
Pine Tribe, 2013.

Østergaard, Erik Korsvik. *The Responsive Leader*. London: LID Publishing, 2018.

Osterwalder, Alexander. "The Culture Map: A Systematic & Intentional Tool for Designing Great Company Culture." *Strategyzer*. Last modified 13 October 2015. https://blog.strategyzer.com/posts/2015/10/13/the-culture-map-a-systematic-intentional-tool-for-designing-great-company-culture.

Pink, Daniel H. *Drive: The Surprising Truth about What Motivates Us*. Edinburgh: Canongate, 2009.

Putnam, Robert D. *Bowling Alone: The Collapse and Revival of American Community*. New York: Simon & Schuster, 2000.

Rau, Ted J., and Jerry Koch-Gonzalez. *Many Voices One Song*. Amherst: Sociocracy For All, 2018.

Responsive.Org. 2019. *Responsive Org*. http://www.responsive.org/.

Richman, Mark. Alignment vs. Autonomy, 2014. Accessed 19 September 2019. https://markrichman.com/alignment-vs-autonomy/

Ries, Eric. *The Lean Startup*. New York: Crown Business, 2011.

Ries, Eric. *The Startup Way*. New York: Currency, 2017.

Robertson, Brian J. *Holacracy: The New Management System for a Rapidly Changing World*. London: Penguin, 2016.

Rummler, Geary A., and Alan P. Brache. *Improving Performance: How to Manage the White Space on the Organization Chart*. San Francisco: Jossey-Bass, 1990.

Scaled Agile Inc. "Scaled Agile Framework: SAFe for Lean Enterprises." Last modified 3 October 2018. https://www.scaledagileframework.com.

Scrum.org. "What Is Scrum?" Last modified 2019. https://www.scrum.org/resources/what-is-scrum.

Seligman, Martin. *Flourish: A Visionary New Understanding of Happiness and Well-Being*. New York: Free Press, 2011.

Sinek, Simon. *Start with Why*. London: Penguin, 2009.

Snabe, Jim Hagemann, and Mikael Trolle. *Dreams and Details*. Copenhagen: Gyldendal Business, 2017.

Sociocracy 3.0. "Consent Decision Making." Last modified 27 June 2019. https://patterns.sociocracy30.org/consent-decision-making.html.

Strategyzer. "The Business Model Canvas." Last modified 2019a. https://strategyzer.com/canvas/business-model-canvas.

Strategyzer. "The Value Proposition Canvas." Last modified 2019b. https://strategyzer.com/canvas/value-proposition-canvas.

Sutherland, Jeff. *Scrum: The Art of Doing Twice the Work in Half the Time.* New York: RH Business Books, 2014.

Taleb, Nicholas Nassim. *Antifragile: Things that Gain from Disorder.* New York: Random House, 2012.

Thrive-in Collaboration. "Four Dimensions Addressed by Sociocracy 3.0." Last modified 16 May 2018. https://www.youtube.com/watch?v=z5rSTOxD3FU.

Timms, Perry. *Transformational HR: How Human Resources Can Create Value and Impact Business Strategy.* London: Kogan Page, 2017.

Wheatley, J. Margaret. *Leadership and the New Science: Discovering Order in a Chaotic World.* San Francisco: Berrett-Koehler, 2006.

World Economic Forum. 2018. *The Future of Jobs Report.* https://lingfeiwu.github.io/smallTeams.

Wu, Lingfei, Dashun Wang and James A. Ewans. "Large Teams Develop and Small Teams Disrupt Science and Technology." *Nature* 566 (2019): 378-382.

ENDNOTES

1. I recommend reading part one of *Exponential Organizations* (Ismail et al., 2014), then *The Lean Startup* (Ries, 2011), next part two of *Exponential Organizations* and finally *The Startup Way* (Ries, 2017). These three books form an extensive foundation for reinventing the approach to innovation and long-lasting market presence.

2. The term 'Blue Ocean strategy' is used by W. Chan Kim and Renée Mauborgne, professors at INSEAD and co-directors of the INSEAD Blue Ocean Strategy Institute, in their book by the same name (Kim and Mauborgne, 2015). Companies can succeed by creating 'Blue Oceans' of new market space as opposed to 'Red Oceans', where competitors fight for dominance, the analogy being that an ocean full of competition turns red with blood.

AN INTRODUCTION TO
ERIK KORSVIK ØSTERGAARD

Erik Korsvik Østergaard is a partner in Bloch&Øster-gaard, which he founded in 2014. He earned the degree of master of science from the Technical University of Copenhagen with a thesis in applied mathematics (also known as chaos mathematics) and has graduated in engineering business administration with a diploma in cross-cultural project management.

Erik has worked with leadership, digitalization, strategy, change management and organizational transformation for over 15 years as a manager, project manager and consultant. He has a burning passion for leadership and engagement.

Over recent years, Erik has focused on codifying the mechanisms of the future of work and striving to establish a leadership framework that provides modern organizations and leaders with a fusion of megatrends, theory and real-life practice. This has led to a line of correlated models for strategy execution, innovation in daily life, culture and the networked organization. These models have been validated in many situations in both large, international organizations and scaleup companies. Combined, these models have provided good, measurable results, especially on people analytics.

The four key findings from his work are gathered in his book *The Responsive Leader*, published in 2018 by LID Publishing. It includes three case studies of modern organizations.

Erik acts as a mentor, speaker, inspirator and motivator. He is a regular guest lecturer at Copenhagen Business School and is also a keen jazz pianist, songwriter and singer.